# POEMS 1960–2000

# Books by Fleur Adcock

POETRY

*The Eye of the Hurricane* (Reed, New Zealand, 1964)
*Tigers* (Oxford University Press, 1967)
*High Tide in the Garden* (Oxford University Press, 1971)
*The Scenic Route* (Oxford University Press, 1974)
*The Inner Harbour* (Oxford University Press, 1979)
*Below Loughrigg* (Bloodaxe Books, 1979)
*Selected Poems* (Oxford University Press, 1983)
*Hotspur: a ballad for music* (Bloodaxe Books, 1986)
*The Incident Book* (Oxford University Press, 1986)
*Meeting the Comet* (Bloodaxe Books, 1988)
*Time-Zones* (Oxford University Press, 1991)
*Looking Back* (Oxford University Press, 1997)
*Poems 1960-2000* (Bloodaxe Books, 2000)

EDITOR

*The Oxford Book of Contemporary New Zealand Poetry*
 (Oxford University Press, 1982)
*The Faber Book of Twentieth Century Women's Poetry*
 (Faber, 1987)
*The Oxford Book of Creatures*, with Jacqueline Simms
 (Oxford University Press, 1995)

EDITOR & TRANSLATOR

*Hugh Primas and the Archpoet*
 (Cambridge University Press, 1994)

TRANSLATOR

*The Virgin & the Nightingale: medieval Latin lyrics*
 (Bloodaxe Books, 1983)
Grete Tartler: *Orient Express*
 (Oxford University Press, 1989)
Daniela Crasnaru: *Letters from Darkness*
 (Oxford University Press, 1991)

# *Fleur Adcock*

# POEMS

# 1960-2000

## BLOODAXE BOOKS

ISBN: 1 85224 529 8 hardback edition
       1 85224 530 1 paperback edition

First published 2000 by
Bloodaxe Books Ltd,
P.O. Box 1SN,
Newcastle upon Tyne NE99 1SN.

Bloodaxe Books Ltd acknowledges
the financial assistance of Northern Arts.

Cover printing by J. Thomson Colour Printers Ltd, Glasgow.

Printed in Great Britain by
Cromwell Press Ltd, Trowbridge, Wiltshire.

# CONTENTS

EARLY POEMS FROM
*The Eye of the Hurricane* (1964) AND *Tigers* (1967)

14 Note on Propertius
15 Flight, with Mountains
17 Beauty Abroad
18 Knife-play
19 Instructions to Vampires
19 Incident
20 Unexpected Visit
21 For Andrew
21 For a Five-Year-Old
22 Comment
22 Miss Hamilton in London
23 The Man Who X-Rayed an Orange
24 Composition for Words and Paint
25 Regression
26 I Ride on My High Bicycle
27 Parting Is Such Sweet Sorrow
28 Hauntings
29 Advice to a Discarded Lover
30 The Water Below
31 Think Before You Shoot
32 The Pangolin

*High Tide in the Garden* (1971)

34 A Game
35 Bogyman
36 Clarendon Whatmough
38 A Surprise in the Peninsula
39 Purple Shining Lilies
40 Afterwards
40 Happy Ending
41 Being Blind
42 Grandma
43 Ngauranga Gorge Hill
44 Stewart Island
44 On a Son Returned to New Zealand
45 Saturday
47 Trees
48 Country Station
49 The Three-toed Sloth
49 Against Coupling
50 Mornings After
52 Gas

## The Scenic Route (1974)

60 The Bullaun
61 Please Identify Yourself
62 Richey
62 The Voyage Out
63 Train from the Hook of Holland
64 Nelia
64 Moa Point
65 Briddes
65 The Famous Traitor
66 Script
68 In Memoriam: James K. Baxter
69 St John's School
70 Pupation
70 The Drought Breaks
71 Kilpeck
72 Feverish
73 Folie à Deux
74 Acris Hiems
75 December Morning
76 Showcase
76 Over the Edge
77 The Net
77 An Illustration to Dante
77 Tokens
78 Naxal
79 Bodnath
80 External Service
80 Flying Back
81 Near Creeslough
82 Kilmacrenan
82 Glenshane

## The Inner Harbour (1979)

### Beginnings

84 Future Work
85 Our Trip to the Federation
86 Mr Morrison
87 Things
87 A Way Out
88 Prelude
89 Accidental
89 A Message
90 Proposal for a Survey
92 Fairy-tale
92 At the Creative Writing Course

*Endings*

93   The Ex-Queen Among the Astronomers
94   Off the Track
94   Beaux Yeux
95   Send-off
95   In Focus
96   Letter from Highgate Wood
97   Poem Ended by a Death
98   Having No Mind for the Same Poem
99   Syringa

*The Thing Itself*

100   Dry Spell
100   Visited
101   The Soho Hospital for Women
103   Variations on a Theme of Horace
105   A Walk in the Snow
105   A Day in October
107   House-talk
107   Foreigner
108   In the Dingle Peninsula
108   In the Terai
109   River

*To and Fro*

110   The Inner Harbour
111   Immigrant
112   Settlers
113   Going Back
115   Instead of an Interview
116   Londoner
116   To Marilyn from London

*Below Loughrigg* (1979)

118   Below Loughrigg
119   Three Rainbows in One Morning
119   Binoculars
120   Paths
120   Mid-point
121   The Spirit of the Place
121   The Vale of Grasmere
122   Letter to Alistair Campbell
123   Declensions
124   Weathering
124   Going Out from Ambleside

## Selected Poems (1983)

128   In the Unicorn, Ambleside
128   Downstream
129   The Hillside
129   This Ungentle Music
130   The Ring
130   Corrosion
131   4 May 1979
131   Madmen
132   Shakespeare's Hotspur
132   Nature Table
133   Revision
134   Influenza
135   Crab
135   Eclipse
136   On the Border
136   The Prize-winning Poem
137   An Emblem
138   Piano Concerto in E Flat Major
139   Villa Isola Bella
140   Lantern Slides
141   Dreaming
142   Street Song
142   Across the Moor
143   Bethan and Bethany
143   Blue Glass
145   Mary Magdalene and the Birds

## Hotspur (1986)

148   Hotspur
153   *Notes*

## The Incident Book (1986)

156   Uniunea Scriitorilor
156   Leaving the Tate
157   The Bedroom Window
158   The Chiffonier
159   Tadpoles
161   For Heidi with Blue Hair
162   The Keepsake
163   England's Glory
164   The Genius of Surrey
165   Loving Hitler

*Schools*

166    Halfway Street, Sidcup
166    St Gertrude's, Sidcup
166    Scalford School
167    Salfords, Surrey
168    Outwood
169    On the School Bus
169    Earlswood
170    Scalford Again
170    Neston
171    Chippenham
172    Tunbridge Wells
173    The High Tree

*Telling Tales*

174    Drowning
175    'Personal Poem'
176    An Epitaph
176    Being Taken from the Place
177    Accidents
177    On the Land
178    Icon
179    Drawings
179    The Telephone Call

*Incidentals*

181    Excavations
182    Pastoral
182    Kissing
183    Double-take
184    Choices

*Thatcherland*

185    Street Scene, London N2
186    Gentlemen's Hairdressers
187    Post Office
188    Demonstration
189    Witnesses
190    Last Song

***Time-Zones*** (1991)

192    Counting
193    Libya
193    What May Happen
194    My Father
195    Cattle in Mist
196    Toads

197 Under the Lawn
198 Wren Song
199 Next Door
200 Heliopsis Scabra
200 House-martins
201 Wildlife
202 Turnip-heads
203 The Batterer
203 Roles
204 Happiness
204 Coupling
204 The Greenhouse Effect
205 The Last Moa
206 Creosote
206 Central Time
208 The Breakfast Program
209 From the Demolition Zone
210 On the Way to the Castle
211 Romania

*Causes*

212 The Farm
213 Aluminium
214 A Hymn to Friendship
215 Smokers for Celibacy

217 *Mrs Fraser's Frenzy*

222 *Meeting the Comet*

**Looking Back** (1997)

I
234 Where They Lived
234 Framed
235 The Russian War
236 227 Peel Green Road
237 Nellie
238 Mary Derry
240 Moses Lambert: the Facts
240 Samuel Joynson
241 Amelia
242 Barber
242 Flames
243 Water
243 A Haunting
244 The Wars
245 Sub Sepibus

246  Anne Welby
247  Beanfield
247  Ancestor to Devotee
248  Frances
250  At Great Hampden
251  At Baddesley Clinton
252  Traitors
254  Swings and Roundabouts
255  Peter Wentworth in Heaven
256  *Notes*

II

257  Tongue Sandwiches
258  The Pilgrim Fathers
259  Paremata
259  Camping
260  Bed and Breakfast
261  Rats
261  Stockings
262  A Political Kiss
262  An Apology
263  Festschrift
263  Offerings
264  Danger: Swimming and Boating Prohibited
265  Risks
265  Blue Footprints in the Snow
266  Summer in Bucharest
267  Moneymore
267  The Voices
268  Willow Creek
269  Giggling
269  Trio
270  The Video

*New Poems* (2000)

272  Easter
272  High Society
273  For Meg
274  A Visiting Angel
275  It's Done This
276  *Kensington Gardens*

281  INDEX OF TITLES AND FIRST LINES

# ACKNOWLEDGEMENTS

This book includes all the poems from Fleur Adcock's *Selected Poems* (Oxford University Press, 1983), which drew upon her earlier OUP collections, *Tigers* (1967), *High Tide in the Garden* (1971), *The Scenic Route* (1974) and *The Inner Harbour* (1979), and *Below Loughrigg* (Bloodaxe Books, 1979), as well as all the poems from her three later OUP collections, *The Incident Book* (1986), *Time-Zones* (1991) and *Looking Back* (1997). It also includes the text of *Hotspur*, a ballad for music by Gillian Whitehead, originally published with monoprints by Gretchen Albrecht (Bloodaxe Books, 1986), and *Meeting the Comet* (Bloodaxe Books, 1988).

Acknowledgements are due to the editors of the following publications in which some of the previously uncollected poems in the *New Poems* section first appeared: *Landfall, Last Words* (Picador, 1999), *Poetry Ireland, Poetry Review* and *Salt*. 'A Visiting Angel' was commissioned by Salisbury Festival for the Last Words project in 1999. Fleur Adcock wishes to thank Royal Park Enterprises and the staff of Kensington Gardens for a Poetry Placement in the summer of 1999.

*early poems from*

# THE EYE OF THE HURRICANE

(1964)

# *and*

# TIGERS

(1967)

## Note on Propertius

Among the Roman love-poets, possession
is a rare theme. The locked and flower-hung door,
the shivering lover, are allowed. To more
buoyant moods, the canons of expression
gave grudging sanction. Do we, then, assume,
finding Propertius tear-sodden and jealous,
that Cynthia was inexorably callous?
Plenty of moonlight entered that high room
whose doors had met his Alexandrine battles;
and she, so gay a lutanist, was known
to stitch and doze a night away, alone,
until the poet tumbled in with apples
for penitence and for her head his wreath,
brought from a party, of wine-scented roses –
(the garland's aptness lying, one supposes,
less in the flowers than in the thorns beneath:
her waking could, he knew, provide his verses
with less idyllic themes). Onto her bed
he rolled the round fruit, and adorned her head;
then gently roused her sleeping mouth to curses.
Here the conventions reassert their power:
the apples fall and bruise, the roses wither,
touched by a sallowed moon. But there were other
luminous nights – (even the cactus flower
glows briefly golden, fed by spiny flesh) –
and once, as he acknowledged, all was singing:
the moonlight musical, the darkness clinging,
and she compliant to his every wish.

# Flight, with Mountains

*(in memory of David Herron)*

### 1

Tarmac, take-off: metallic words conduct us
over that substance, black with spilt rain,
to this event. Sealed, we turn and pause.
Engines churn and throb to a climax, then
up: a hard spurt, and the passionate rise
levels out for this gradual incline.

There was something of pleasure in that thrust
from earth into ignorant cloud; but here,
above all tremors of sensation, rest
replaces motion; secretly we enter
the obscurely gliding current, and encased
in vitreous calm inhabit the high air.

Now I see, beneath the plated wing,
cloud edges withdrawing their slow foam
from shoreline, rippling hills, and beyond, the long
crested range of the land's height. I am
carried too far by this blind rocketing:
faced with mountains, I remember him

whose death seems a convention of such a view:
another one for the mountains. Another one
who, climbing to stain the high snow
with his shadow, fell, and briefly caught between
sudden earth and sun, projected below
a flicker of darkness; as, now, this plane.

### 2

Only air to hold the wings;
only words to hold the story;
only a frail web of cells
to hold heat in the body.

Breath bleeds from throat and lungs
under the last cold fury;
words wither; meaning fails;
steel wings grow heavy.

3

Headlines announced it, over a double column of type:
the cabled facts, public regret, and a classified list
of your attainments – degrees, scholarships and positions,
and notable feats of climbing. So the record stands:
no place there for my private annotations. The face
that smiles in some doubt from a fuscous half-tone block
stirs me hardly more than those I have mistaken
daily, about the streets, for yours.
                                                I can refer
to my own pictures; and turning first to the easiest,
least painful, I see Dave the raconteur,
playing a shoal of listeners on a casual line
of dry narration. Other images unreel:
your face in a car, silent, watching the dark road,
or animated and sunburnt from your hard pleasures
of snow and rock-face; again, I see you arguing,
practical and determined, as you draw with awkward puffs
at a rare cigarette.
                        So much, in vivid sequence
memory gives. And then, before I can turn away,
imagination adds the last scene: your eyes bruised,
mouth choked under a murderous weight of snow.


4

*'When you reach the top of a mountain, keep on climbing'* –
meaning, we may suppose,
to sketch on space the cool arabesques of birds
in plastic air, or those
exfoliating arcs, upward and outward,
of an aeronautic show.
Easier, such a free fall in reverse,
higher than clogging snow
or clutching gravity, than the awkward local
embrace of rocks. And observe
the planets coursing their elliptical race-tracks,
where each completed curve
cinctures a new dimension. Mark these patterns.
Mark, too, how the high
air thins. The top of any mountain
is a base for the sky.

**5**

Further by days and oceans than all my flying
you have gone, while here the air insensibly flowing
over a map of mountains drowns my dumbness.
A turn of the earth away, where a crawling dimness
waits now to absorb our light, another
snowscape, named like this one, took you; and neither
rope, nor crumbling ice, nor your unbelieving
uncommitted hands could hold you to living.
Wheels turn; the dissolving air rolls over
an arc of thunder. Gone is gone forever.


## Beauty Abroad

Carrying still the dewy rose
for which she's bound to payment, Beauty goes
trembling through the gruesome wood:
small comfort to her that she's meek and good.
A branch cracks, and the beast appears:
she sees the fangs, the eyes, the bristly ears,
stifles a scream, and smooths her dress;
but his concern is for his own distress.
He lays his muzzle on her hand,
says 'Pity me!' and 'Can you understand?
Be kind!' And then goes on to praise
her pretty features and her gentle ways.
Beauty inclines a modest ear,
hears what she has decided she should hear,
and with no thought to ask 'What then?'
follows the creature to his hairy den.
The beast, like any hero, knows
sweet talk can lead him to *la belle chose*.

# Knife-play

All my scars are yours. We talk of pledges,
and holding out my hand I show
the faint burn on the palm and the hair-thin
razor-marks at wrist and elbow:

self-inflicted, yes; but your tokens —
made as distraction from a more
inaccessible pain than could have been
caused by cigarette or razor —

and these my slightest marks. In all our meetings
you were the man with the long knives,
piercing the living hopes, cutting connections,
carving and dissecting motives,

and with an expert eye for dagger-throwing:
a showman's aim. Oh, I could dance
and dodge, as often as not, the whistling blades,
turning on a brave performance

to empty stands. I leaned upon a hope
that this might prove to have been less
a gladiatorial show, contrived for murder,
than a formal test of fitness

(initiation rites are always painful)
to bring me ultimately to your
regard. Well, in a sense it was; for now
I have found some kind of favour:

you have learnt softness; I, by your example,
am well-schooled in contempt; and while
you speak of truce I laugh, and to your pleading
turn a cool and guarded profile.

I have now, you might say, the upper hand:
these knives that bristle in my flesh
increase my armoury and lessen yours.
I can pull out, whet and polish

your weapons, and return to the attack,
well-armed. It is a pretty trick,
but one that offers little consolation.
such a victory would be Pyrrhic,

occurring when my strength is almost spent.
No: I would make an end of fighting
and, bleeding as I am from old wounds,
die like the bee upon a sting.


## Instructions to Vampires

I would not have you drain
with your sodden lips the flesh that has fed mine,
and leech his bubbling blood to a decline:
not that pain;

nor visit on his mind
that other desiccation, where the wit
shrivels: so to be humbled in not fit
for his kind.

But use acid or flame,
secretly, to brand or cauterise;
and on the soft globes of his mortal eyes
etch my name.


## Incident

When you were lying on the white sand,
a rock under your head, and smiling,
(circled by dead shells), I came to you
and you said, reaching to take my hand,
'Lie down.' So for a time we lay
warm on the sand, talking and smoking,
easy; while the grovelling sea behind
sucked at the rocks and measured the day.
Lightly I fell asleep then, and fell
into a cavernous dream of falling.
It was all the cave-myths, it was all
the myths of tunnel or tower or well –
Alice's rabbit-hole into the ground,
or the path of Orpheus: a spiral staircase
to hell, furnished with danger and doubt.

Stumbling, I suddenly woke; and found
water about me. My hair was wet,
and you were lying on the grey sand
waiting for the lapping tide to take me:
watching, and lighting a cigarette.


## Unexpected Visit


I have nothing to say about this garden.
I do not want to be here, I can't explain
what happened. I merely opened a usual door
and found this. The rain

has just stopped, and the gravel paths are trickling
with water. Stone lions, on each side,
gleam like wet seals, and the green birds
are stiff with dripping pride.

Not my kind of country. The gracious vistas,
the rose-gardens and terraces, are all wrong –
as comfortless as the weather. But here I am.
I cannot tell how long

I have stood gazing at grass too wet to sit on,
under a sky so dull I cannot read
the sundial, staring along the curving walks
and wondering where they lead;

not really hoping, though, to be enlightened.
It must be morning, I think, but there is no
horizon behind the trees, no sun as clock
or compass. I shall go

and find, somewhere among the formal hedges
or hidden behind a trellis, a toolshed. There
I can sit on a box and wait. Whatever happens
may happen anywhere,

and better, perhaps, among the rakes and flowerpots
and sacks of bulbs than under this pallid sky:
having chosen nothing else, I can at least
choose to be warm and dry.

## For Andrew

'Will I die?' you ask. And so I enter on
the dutiful exposition of that which you
would rather not know, and I rather not tell you.
To soften my 'Yes' I offer compensations –
age and fulfilment ('It's so far away;
you will have children and grandchildren by then')
and indifference ('By then you will not care').
No need: you cannot believe me, convinced
that if you always eat plenty of vegetables
and are careful crossing the street you will live for ever.
And so we close the subject, with much unsaid –
this, for instance: Though you and I may die
tomorrow or next year, and nothing remain
of our stock, of the unique, preciously-hoarded
inimitable genes we carry in us,
it is possible that for many generations
there will exist, sprung from whatever seeds,
children straight-limbed, with clear enquiring voices,
bright-eyed as you. Or so I like to think:
sharing in this your childish optimism.


## For a Five-Year-Old

A snail is climbing up the window-sill
into your room, after a night of rain.
You call me in to see, and I explain
that it would be unkind to leave it there:
it might crawl to the floor; we must take care
that no one squashes it. You understand,
and carry it outside, with careful hand,
to eat a daffodil.

I see, then, that a kind of faith prevails:
your gentleness is moulded still by words
from me, who have trapped mice and shot wild birds,
from me, who drowned your kittens, who betrayed
your closest relatives, and who purveyed
the harshest kind of truth to many another.
But that is how things are: I am your mother,
and we are kind to snails.

# Comment

The four-year-old believes he likes
vermouth; the cat eats cheese;
and you and I, though scarcely more
convincingly than these,
walk in the gardens, hand in hand,
beneath the summer trees.


# Miss Hamilton in London

It would not be true to say she was doing nothing:
she visited several bookshops, spent an hour
in the Victoria and Albert Museum (Indian section),
and walked carefully through the streets of Kensington
carrying five mushrooms in a paper bag,
a tin of black pepper, a literary magazine,
and enough money to pay the rent for two weeks.
The sky was cloudy, leaves lay on the pavements.

Nor did she lack human contacts: she spoke
to three shop-assistants and a newsvendor,
and returned the 'Goodnight' of a museum attendant.
Arriving home, she wrote a letter to someone
in Canada, as it might be, or in New Zealand,
listened to the news as she cooked her meal,
and conversed for five minutes with the landlady.
The air was damp with the mist of late autumn.

A full day, and not unrewarding.
Night fell at the usual seasonal hour.
She drew the curtains, switched on the electric fire,
washed her hair and read until it was dry,
then went to bed; where, for the hours of darkness,
she lay pierced by thirty black spears
and felt her limbs numb, her eyes burning,
and dark rust carried along her blood.

# The Man Who X-Rayed an Orange

Viewed from the top, he said, it was like a wheel,
the paper-thin spokes raying out from the hub
to the half-transparent circumference of rind,
with small dark ellipses suspended between.
He could see the wood of the table-top through it.
Then he knelt, and with his eye at orange-level
saw it as the globe, its pithy core
upright from pole to flattened pole. Next,
its levitation: sustained (or so he told us)
by a week's diet of nothing but rice-water
he had developed powers, drawing upon which
he raised it to a height of about two feet
above the table, with never a finger near it.
That was all. It descended, gradually opaque,
to rest; while he sat giddy and shivering.
(He shivered telling it.) But surely, we asked,
(and still none of us mentioned self-hypnosis
or hallucinations caused by lack of food),
surely triumphant too? Not quite, he said,
with his little crooked smile. It was not enough:
he should have been able to summon up,
created out of what he had newly learnt,
a perfectly imaginary orange, complete
in every detail; whereupon the real orange
would have vanished. Then came explanations
and his talk of mysticism, occult physics,
alchemy, the Qabalah – all his hobby-horses.
If there was failure, it was only here
in the talking. For surely he had lacked nothing,
neither power nor insight nor imagination,
when he knelt alone in his room, seeing before him
suspended in the air that golden globe,
visible and transparent, light-filled:
his only fruit from the Tree of Life.

# Composition for Words and Paint

This darkness has a quality
that poses us in shapes and textures,
one plane behind another,
flatness in depth.

Your face; a fur of hair; a striped
curtain behind, and to one side cushions;
nothing recedes, all lies extended.
I sink upon your image.

I see a soft metallic glint,
a tinsel weave behind the canvas,
aluminium and bronze beneath the ochre.
There is more in this than we know.

I can imagine drawn around you
a white line, in delicate brush-strokes:
emphasis; but you do not need it.
You have completeness.

I am not measuring your gestures;
(I have seen you measure those of others,
know a mind by a hand's trajectory,
the curve of a lip).

But you move, and I move towards you,
draw back your head, and I advance.
I am fixed to the focus of your eyes.
I share your orbit.

Now I discover things about you:
your thin wrists, a tooth missing;
and how I melt and burn before you.
I have known you always.

The greyness from the long windows
reduces visual depth; but tactile
reality defies half-darkness.
My hands prove you solid.

You draw me down upon your body,
hard arms behind my head.
Darkness and soft colours blur.
We have swallowed the light.

Now I dissolve you in my mouth,
catch in the corners of my throat
the sly taste of your love, sliding
into me, singing;

just as the birds have started singing.
Let them come flying through the windows
with chains of opals around their necks.
We are expecting them.


## Regression


All the flowers have gone back into the ground.
We fell on them, and they did not lie
crushed and crumpled, waiting to die
on the earth's surface. No: they suddenly wound

the film of their growth backwards. We saw them shrink
from blossom to bud to tiny shoot,
down from the stem and up from the root.
Back to the seed, brothers. It makes you think.

Clearly they do not like us. They've gone away,
given up. And who could blame
anything else for doing the same?
I notice that certain trees look smaller today.

You can't escape the fact: there's a backward trend
from oak to acorn, and from pine
to cone; they all want to resign.
Understandable enough, but where does it end?

Harder, you'd think, for animals; yet the cat
was pregnant, but has not produced.
Her rounded belly is reduced,
somehow, to normal. How to answer that?

Buildings, perhaps, will be the next to go;
imagine it: a tinkle of glass,
a crunch of brick, and a house will pass
through the soil to the protest meeting below.

This whole conspiracy of inverted birth
leaves only us; and how shall we
endure as we deserve to be,
foolish and lost on the naked skin of the earth?


## I Ride on My High Bicycle

I ride on my high bicycle
into a sooty Victorian city
of colonnaded bank buildings,
horse-troughs, and green marble fountains.

I glide along, contemplating
the curly lettering on the shop-fronts.
An ebony elephant, ten feet tall,
is wheeled past, advertising something.

When I reach the dark archway
I chain my bicycle to a railing,
nod to a policeman, climb the steps,
and emerge into unexpected sunshine.

There below lies Caroline Bay,
its red roofs and its dazzling water.
Now I am running along the path;
it is four o'clock, there is still just time.

I halt and sit on the sandy grass
to remove my shoes and thick stockings;
but something has caught me; around my shoulders
I feel barbed wire; I am entangled.

It pulls my hair, dragging me downwards;
I am suddenly older than seventeen,
tired, powerless, pessimistic.
I struggle weakly; and wake, of course.

Well, all right. It doesn't matter.
Perhaps I didn't get to the beach:
but I have been there – to all the beaches
(waking or dreaming) and all the cities.

Now it is very early morning
and from my window I see a leopard
tall as a horse, majestic and kindly,
padding over the fallen snow.


## Parting Is Such Sweet Sorrow


The room is full of clichés – 'Throw me a crumb'
and 'Now I see the writing on the wall'
and 'Don't take umbrage, dear'. I wish I could.
Instead I stand bedazzled by them all,

longing for shade. Belshazzar's fiery script
glows there, between the prints of tropical birds,
in neon lighting, and the air is full
of crumbs that flash and click about me. Words

glitter in colours like those gaudy prints:
the speech of a computer, metal-based
but feathered like a cloud of darts. All right.
Your signal-system need not go to waste.

Mint me another batch of tokens: say
'I am in your hands; I throw myself upon
your mercy, casting caution to the winds.'
Thank you; there is no need to go on.

Thus authorised by your mechanical
issue, I lift you like a bale of hay,
open the window wide, and toss you out;
and gales of laughter whirl you far away.

# Hauntings

Three times I have slept in your house
and this is definitely the last.
I cannot endure the transformations:
nothing stays the same for an hour.

Last time there was a spiral staircase
winding across the high room.
People tramped up and down it all night,
carrying brief-cases, pails of milk, bombs,

pretending not to notice me
as I lay in a bed lousy with dreams.
Couldn't you have kept them away?
After all, they were trespassing.

The time before it was all bathrooms,
full of naked, quarrelling girls –
and you claim to like solitude:
I do not understand your arrangements.

Now the glass doors to the garden
open on rows of stone columns;
beside them stands a golden jeep.
Where are we this time? On what planet?

Every night lasts for a week.
I toss and turn and wander about,
whirring from room to room like a moth,
ignored by those indifferent faces.

At last I think I have woken up.
I lift my head from the pillow, rejoicing.
The alarm-clock is playing Schubert:
I am still asleep. This is too much.

Well, I shall try again in a minute.
I shall wake into this real room
with its shadowy plants and patterned screens
(yes, I remember how it looks).

It will be cool, but I shan't wait
to light the gas-fire. I shall dress
(I know where my clothes are) and slip out.
You needn't think I am here to stay.

# Advice to a Discarded Lover

Think, now: if you have found a dead bird,
not only dead, not only fallen,
but full of maggots: what do you feel –
more pity or more revulsion?

Pity is for the moment of death,
and the moments after. It changes
when decay comes, with the creeping stench
and the wriggling, munching scavengers.

Returning later, though, you will see
a shape of clean bone, a few feathers,
an inoffensive symbol of what
once lived. Nothing to make you shudder.

It is clear then. But perhaps you find
the analogy I have chosen
for our dead affair rather gruesome –
too unpleasant a comparison.

It is not accidental. In you
I see maggots close to the surface.
You are eaten up by self-pity,
crawling with unlovable pathos.

If I were to touch you I should feel
against my fingers fat, moist worm-skin.
Do not ask me for charity now:
go away until your bones are clean.

# The Water Below

This house is floored with water,
wall to wall, a deep green pit,
still and gleaming, edged with stone.
Over it are built stairways
and railed living-areas
in wrought iron. All rather
impractical; it will be
damp in winter, and we shall
surely drop small objects – keys,
teaspoons, or coins – through the chinks
in the ironwork, to splash
lost into the glimmering
depths (and do we know how deep?).
It will have to be rebuilt:
a solid floor of concrete
over this dark well (perhaps
already full of coins, like
the flooded crypt of that church
in Ravenna). You might say
it could be drained, made into
a useful cellar for coal.
But I am sure the water
would return; would never go.
Under my grandmother's house
in Drury, when I was three,
I always believed there was
water: lift up the floorboards
and you would see it – a lake,
a subterranean sea.
True, I played under the house
and saw only hard-packed earth,
wooden piles, gardening tools,
a place to hunt for lizards.
That was different: below
I saw no water. Above,
I knew it must still be there,
waiting. (For why did we say
'Forgive us our trespasses,
deliver us from evil'?)
Always beneath the safe house
lies the pool, the hidden sea
created before we were.
It is not easy to drain
the waters under the earth.

# Think Before You Shoot

Look, children, the wood is full of tigers,
scorching the bluebells with their breath.
You reach for guns. Will you preserve the flowers
at such cost? Will you prefer the death
of prowling stripes to a mush of trampled stalks?
Through the eyes, then – do not spoil the head.
Tigers are easier to shoot than to like.
Sweet necrophiles, you only love them dead.

There now, you've got three – and with such fur, too,
golden and warm and salty. Very good.
Don't expect them to forgive you, though.
There are plenty more of them. This is their wood
(and their bluebells, which you have now forgotten).
They've eaten all the squirrels. They want you,
and it's no excuse to say you're only children.
No one is on your side. What will you do?

## The Pangolin

There have been all those tigers, of course,
and a leopard, and a six-legged giraffe,
and a young deer that ran up to my window
before it was killed, and once a blue horse,
and somewhere an impression of massive dogs.
Why do I dream of such large, hot-blooded beasts
covered with sweating fur and full of passions
when there could be dry lizards and cool frogs,
or slow, modest creatures, as a rest
from all those panting, people-sized animals?
Hedgehogs or perhaps tortoises would do,
but I think the pangolin would suit me best:
a vegetable animal, who goes
disguised as an artichoke or asparagus-tip
in a green coat of close-fitting leaves,
with his flat shovel-tail and his pencil-nose:
the scaly anteater. Yes, he would fit
more aptly into a dream than into his cage
in the Small Mammal House; so I invite him
to be dreamt about, if he would care for it.

# HIGH TIDE IN THE GARDEN

(1971)

## A Game

They are throwing the ball
to and fro between them,
in and out of the picture.
She is in the painting
hung on the wall
in a narrow gold frame.
He stands on the floor
catching and tossing
at the right distance.
She wears a white dress,
black boots and stockings,
and a flowered straw hat.
She moves in silence
but it seems from her face
that she must be laughing.
Behind her is sunlight
and a tree-filled garden;
you might think to hear
birds or running water,
but no, there is nothing.
Once or twice he has spoken
but does so no more,
for she cannot answer.
So he stands smiling,
playing her game
(she is almost a child),
not daring to go,
intent on the ball.
And she is the same.
For what would result
neither wishes to know
if it should fall.

# Bogyman

Stepping down from the blackberry bushes
he stands in my path: Bogyman.
He is not as I had remembered him,
though he still wears the broad-brimmed hat,
the rubber-soled shoes and the woollen gloves.
No face; and that soft mooning voice
still spinning its endless distracting yarn.

But this is daylight, a misty autumn
Sunday, not unpopulated
by birds. I can see him in such colours
as he wears – fawn, grey, murky blue –
not all shadow-clothed, as he was that night
when I was ten; he seems less tall
(I have grown) and less muffled in silence.

I have no doubt at all, though, that he is
Bogyman. He is why children
do not sleep all night in their tree-houses.
He is why, when I had pleaded
to spend a night on the common, under
a cosy bush, and my mother
surprisingly said yes, she took no risk.

He was the risk I would not take; better
to make excuses, to lose face,
than to meet the really faceless, the one
whose name was too childish for us
to utter – 'murderers' we talked of, and
'lunatics escaped from Earlswood'.
But I met him, of course, as we all do.

Well, that was then; I survived; and later
survived meetings with his other
forms, bold or pathetic or disguised – the
slummocking figure in a dark
alley, or the lover turned suddenly
icy-faced; fingers at my throat
and ludicrous violence in kitchens.

I am older now, and (I tell myself,
circling carefully around him
at the far edge of the path, pretending
I am not in fact confronted)
can deal with such things. But what, Bogyman,
shall I be at twice my age? (At
your age?) Shall I be grandmotherly, fond

suddenly of gardening, chatty with
neighbours? Or strained, not giving in,
writing for *Ambit* and hitch-hiking to
Turkey? Or sipping Guinness in
the Bald-Faced Stag, in wrinkled stockings? Or
(and now I look for the first time
straight at you) something like you, Bogyman?


## Clarendon Whatmough


Clarendon Whatmough sits in his chair
telling me that I am hollow.
The walls of his study are dark and bare;
he has his back to the window.
Are you priest or psychiatrist, Clarendon Whatmough?
I do not have to believe you.

The priest in the pub kept patting my hand
more times than I thought needful.
I let him think me a Catholic, and
giggled, and felt quite sinful.
You were not present, Clarendon Whatmough:
I couldn't have flirted with you.

Christopher is no longer a saint
but I still carry the medal
with his image on, which my mother sent
to protect me when I travel.
It pleases her – and me: two
unbelievers, Clarendon Whatmough.

But when a friend was likely to die
I wanted to pray, if I could
after so many years, and feeling shy
of churches walked in the wood.
A hypocritical thing to do,
would you say, Clarendon Whatmough?

Or a means of dispelling buried guilt,
a conventional way to ease
my fears? I tell you this: I felt
the sky over the trees
crack open like a nutshell. You
don't believe me, Clarendon Whatmough:

or rather, you would explain that I
induced some kind of reaction
to justify the reversal of my
usual lack of conviction.
No comment from Clarendon Whatmough.
He tells me to continue.

Why lay such critical emphasis
on this other-worldly theme?
I could tell you my sexual fantasies
as revealed in my latest dream.
Do, if you wish, says Clarendon Whatmough:
it's what I expect of you.

Clarendon Whatmough doesn't sneer;
he favours a calm expression,
prefers to look lofty and austere
and let me display an emotion
then anatomise it. Clarendon Whatmough,
shall I analyse you?

No: that would afford me even less
amusement than I provide.
We may both very well be centreless,
but I will not look inside
your shadowy eyes; nor shall you
now, in my open ones, Clarendon Whatmough.

I leave you fixed in your formal chair,
your ambiguous face unseeing,
and go, thankful that I'm aware
at least of my own being.
Who is convinced, though, Clarendon Whatmough,
of your existence? Are you?

## A Surprise in the Peninsula

When I came in that night I found
the skin of a dog stretched flat and
nailed upon my wall between the
two windows. It seemed freshly killed –
there was blood at the edges. Not
my dog: I have never owned one,
I rather dislike them. (Perhaps
whoever did it knew that.) It
was a light brown dog, with smooth hair;
no head, but the tail still remained.
On the flat surface of the pelt
was branded the outline of the
peninsula, singed in thick black
strokes into the fur: a coarse map.
The position of the town was
marked by a bullet-hole; it went
right through the wall. I placed my eye
to it, and could see the dark trees
outside the house, flecked with moonlight.
I locked the door then, and sat up
all night, drinking small cups of the
bitter local coffee. A dog
would have been useful, I thought, for
protection. But perhaps the one
I had been given performed that
function; for no one came that night,
nor for three more. On the fourth day
it was time to leave. The dog-skin
still hung on the wall, stiff and dry
by now, the flies and the smell gone.
Could it, I wondered, have been meant
not as a warning, but a gift?
And, scarcely shuddering, I drew
the nails out and took it with me.

## Purple Shining Lilies

The events of the *Aeneid* were not enacted
on a porridge-coloured plain; although my
greyish pencilled-over Oxford text
is monochrome, tends to deny
the flaming pyre, that fearful tawny light,
the daily colour-productions in the sky

(dawn variously rosy); Charon's boat
mussel-shell blue on the reedy mud
of Styx; the wolf-twins in a green cave;
huge Triton rising from the flood
to trumpet on his sky-coloured conch;
and everywhere the gleam of gold and blood.

Cybele's priest rode glittering into battle
on a bronze-armoured horse: his great bow
of gold, his cloak saffron, he himself
splendid in *ferrugine et ostro* –
rust and shellfish. (We laugh, but Camilla
for this red and purple gear saw fit to go

to her death.) The names, indeed, are as foreign
in their resonances as the battle-rite:
*luteus* with its vaguely medical air;
grim *ater*; or the two versions of white:
*albus* thick and eggy; *candidus*
clear as a candle-flame's transparent light.

It dazzled me, that white, when I was young;
that and *purpureus* – poppy-red,
scarlet, we were firmly taught, not purple
in the given context; but inside my head
the word was both something more than visual
and also exactly what it said.

Poppies and lilies mixed (the mystical
and the moral?) was what I came upon.
My eyes leaping across the juxtaposed
adjectives, I saw them both as one,
and brooded secretly upon the image:
purple shining lilies, bright in the sun.

We weave haunted circles about each other,
advance and retreat in turn, like witch-doctors
before a fetish. Yes, you are right to fear
me now, and I you. But love, this ritual
will exhaust us. Come closer. Listen. Be brave.
I am going to talk to you quietly
as sometimes, in the long past (you remember?),
we made love. Let us be intent, and still. Still.
There are ways of approaching it. This is one:
this gentle talk, with no pause for suspicion,
no hesitation, because you do not know
the thing is upon you, until it has come –
now, and you did not even hear it.
                              Silence
is what I am trying to achieve for us.
A nothingness, a non-relatedness, this
unknowing into which we are sliding now
together: this will have to be our kingdom.

Rain is falling. Listen to the gentle rain.

## Happy Ending

After they had not made love
she pulled the sheet up over her eyes
until he was buttoning his shirt:
not shyness for their bodies – those
they had willingly displayed – but a frail
endeavour to apologise.

Later, though, drawn together by
a distaste for such 'untidy ends'
they agreed to meet again; whereupon
they giggled, reminisced, held hands
as though what they had made was love –
and not that happier outcome, friends.

# Being Blind

*(for Meg Sheffield)*


Listen to that:
it is the sea rushing across the garden
swamping the apple tree, beating against the house,
carrying white petals; the sea from France
coming to us.
                    It is the April wind
I tell myself, but cannot rise to look.

You were talking about your blind friend –
how you had to share a room with her once
on holiday, and in the night you woke:
she was staring at you. Was she really blind?
You leaned over her bed for a long time,
watching her, trying to understand,
suppressing unworthy, unendurable
speculations (if she could see
what kind of creature was she?) until
her eyes went swivelling in a dream
as ours do, closed. Yes: blind.

Then I came to bed and, thinking of her
for whom eyelids have no particular purpose,
closed mine. And now there is this sound
of a savage tide rushing towards me.
Do you, in the front of the house, hear it?
I cannot look out. I am blind now.
If I walk downstairs, hand on the banister
(as she did once – admiring, she told us,
our Christmas lights), if I open the door
it will swish and swill over my feet:
the sea. Listen.

# Grandma

It was the midnight train; I was tired and edgy.
The advertisement portrayed – I wrote it down – a
'Skull-like young female, licking lips' and I added
'Prefer Grandma, even dead' as she newly was.
I walked home singing one of her Irish ballads.

Death is one thing, necrophilia another.

So I climbed up that ladder in the frescoed barn –
a soft ladder, swaying and collapsing under
my feet (my hands alone hauled me into the loft) –
and found, without surprise, a decomposed lady
who drew me down to her breast, with her disengaged
armbones, saying 'Come, my dearie, don't be afraid,
come to me' into a mess of sweetish decay.

It was a dream. I screamed and woke, put on the light,
dozed, woke again. For half a day I carried that
carcass in my own failing arms. Then remembered:
even the dead want to be loved for their own sake.
She was indeed my grandmother. She did not choose
to be dead and rotten. My blood too (Group A,
Rhesus negative, derived exactly from hers)
will suffer that deterioration; my much
modified version of her nose will fall away,
my longer bones collapse like hers. So let me now
apologise to my sons and their possible
children for the gruesomeness: we do not mean it.

# Ngauranga Gorge Hill

The bee in the foxglove, the mouth on the nipple,
the hand between the thighs.
                              Forgive me
these procreative images.
                         Do you remember
that great hill outside Wellington, which we

had to climb, before they built the motorway,
to go north? The engine used to boil
in the old Chev. Straight up the road went
and tipped us over into Johnsonville.

Nothing on the way but rock and gorse, gravel-
pits, and foxgloves; and a tunnel hacked deep,
somewhere, into a cliff. Ah, my burgeoning new
country, I said (being fourteen). Yes, a steep

road to climb. But coming back was better;
a matter for some caution in a car,
but glorious and terrible on a bicycle.
Heart in my pedals, down I would roar

towards the sea; I'd go straight into it
if I didn't brake. No time then to stare
self-consciously at New Zealand vegetation,
at the awkward landscape. I needed all my care

for making the right turn towards the city
at the hill's base, where the paint-hoarding stood
between me and the harbour.
                            For ten years
that city possessed me. In time it bred

two sons for me (little pink mouths tucked
like foxglove-bells over my nipples). Yes,
in this matter Wellington and I have no
quarrel. But I think it was a barren place.

## Stewart Island

'But look at all this beauty,'
said the hotel manager's wife
when asked how she could bear to
live there. True: there was a fine bay,
all hills and atmosphere; white
sand, and bush down to the sea's edge;
oyster-boats, too, and Maori
fishermen with Scottish names (she
ran off with one that autumn).
As for me, I walked on the beach;
it was too cold to swim. My
seven-year-old collected shells
and was bitten by sandflies;
my four-year-old paddled, until
a mad seagull jetted down
to jab its claws and beak into
his head. I had already
decided to leave the country.

## On a Son Returned to New Zealand

He is my green branch growing in a far plantation.
He is my first invention.

No one can be in two places at once.
So we left Athens on the same morning.
I was in a hot railway carriage, crammed
between Serbian soldiers and peasant
women, on sticky seats, with nothing to
drink but warm mineral water.
                              He was
in a cabin with square windows, sailing
across the Mediterranean, fast,
to Suez.
          Then I was back in London
in the tarnished summer, remembering,
as I folded his bed up, and sent the
television set away. Letters came
from Aden and Singapore, late.

He was
already in his father's house, on the
cliff-top, where the winter storms roll across
from Kapiti Island, and the flax bends
before the wind. He could go no further.

He is my bright sea-bird on a rocky beach.

## Saturday

I am sitting on the step
drinking coffee and
smoking, listening to jazz.
The smoke separates
two scents: fresh paint in the house
behind me; in front,
buddleia.
      The neighbours cut
back our lilac tree –
it shaded their neat garden.
The buddleia will
be next, no doubt; but bees and
all those butterflies
approve of our shaggy trees.

           *

I am painting the front door
with such thick juicy
paint I could almost eat it.
People going past
with their shopping stare at my
bare legs and old shirt.
The door will be sea-green.
          Our
black cat walked across
the painted step and left a
delicate paw-trail.
I swore at her and frightened
two little girls – this
street is given to children.

The other cat is younger,
white and tabby, fat,
with a hoarse voice. In summer
she sleeps all day long
in the rosebay willow-herb,
too lazy to walk
on paint.
          Andrew is upstairs;
having discovered
quick-drying non-drip gloss, he
is old enough now
to paint all his furniture
tangerine and the
woodwork green; he is singing.

                    *

I am lying in the sun,
in the garden. Bees
dive on white clover beside
my ears. The sky is
Greek blue, with a vapour-trail
chalked right across it.
My transistor radio
talks about the moon.

                    *

I am floating in the sky.
Below me the house
crouches among its trees like
a cat in long grass.
I want to stroke its roof-ridge
but I think I can
already hear it purring.

# Trees

Elm, laburnum, hawthorn, oak:
all the incredible leaves expand
on their dusty branches, like
Japanese paper flowers in water,
like anything one hardly believes
will really work this time; and
I am a stupefied spectator
as usual. What are they all, these
multiverdant, variously-made
soft sudden things, these leaves?
So I walk solemnly in the park
with a copy of *Let's Look at Trees*
from the children's library,
identifying leaf-shapes and bark
while behind my back, at home,
my own garden is turning into a wood.
Before my house the pink may tree
lolls its heavy heads over mine
to grapple my hair as I come
in; at the back door I walk out
under lilac. The two elders
(I let them grow for the wine)
hang vastly over the fence, no doubt
infuriating my tidy neighbours.
In the centre the apple tree
needs pruning. And everywhere,
soaring over the garden shed,
camouflaged by roses, or snaking
up through the grass like vertical worms,
grows every size of sycamore.
Last year we attacked them; I saw
my son, so tender to ants, so sad
over dead caterpillars, hacking
at living roots as thick as his arms,
drenching the stumps with creosote.
No use: they continue to grow.
Under the grass, the ground
must be peppered with winged seeds,
meshed with a tough stringy net
of roots; and the house itself undermined
by wandering wood. Shall we see
the floorboards lifted one morning
by these indomitable weeds,

or find in the airing-cupboard
a rather pale sapling?
And if we do, will it be
worse than cracked pipes or dry rot?
Trees I can tolerate; they are why
I chose this house – for the apple tree,
elder, buddleia, lilac, may;
and outside my bedroom window, higher
every week, its leaves unfurling
pink at the twig-tips (composite
in form) the tallest sycamore.

## Country Station

First she made a little garden
of sorrel stalks wedged among
some yellowy-brown moss-cushions

and fenced it with ice-lolly sticks
(there were just enough); then she
set out biscuit-crumbs on a brick

for the ants; now she sits on a
deserted luggage-trolley
to watch them come for their dinner.

It's nice here – cloudy but quite warm.
Five trains have swooshed through, and one
stopped, but at the other platform.

Later, when no one is looking,
she may climb the roof of that
low shed. Her mother is making

another telephone call (she
isn't crying any more).
Perhaps they will stay here all day.

# The Three-toed Sloth

The three-toed sloth is the slowest creature we know
for its size. It spends its life hanging upside-down
from a branch, its baby nestling on its breast.
It never cleans itself, but lets fungus grow
on its fur. The grin it wears, like an idiot clown,
proclaims the joys of a life which is one long rest.

The three-toed sloth is content. It doesn't care.
It moves imperceptibly, like the laziest snail
you ever saw blown up to the size of a sheep.
Disguised as a grey-green bough it dangles there
in the steamy Amazon jungle. That long-drawn wail
is its slow-motion sneeze. Then it falls asleep.

One cannot but envy such torpor. Its top speed,
when rushing to save its young, is a dramatic
fourteen feet per minute, in a race with fate.
The puzzle is this, though: how did nature breed
a race so determinedly unenergetic?
What passion ever inspired a sloth to mate?


# Against Coupling

I write in praise of the solitary act:
of not feeling a trespassing tongue
forced into one's mouth, one's breath
smothered, nipples crushed against the
ribcage, and that metallic tingling
in the chin set off by a certain odd nerve:

unpleasure. Just to avoid those eyes would help –
such eyes as a young girl draws life from,
listening to the vegetal
rustle within her, as his gaze
stirs polypal fronds in the obscure
sea-bed of her body, and her own eyes blur.

There is much to be said for abandoning
this no longer novel exercise –
for not 'participating in
a total experience' – when
one feels like the lady in Leeds who
had seen *The Sound of Music* eighty-six times;

or more, perhaps, like the school drama mistress
producing *A Midsummer Night's Dream*
for the seventh year running, with
yet another cast from 5B.
Pyramus and Thisbe are dead, but
the hole in the wall can still be troublesome.

I advise you, then, to embrace it without
encumbrance. No need to set the scene,
dress up (or undress), make speeches.
Five minutes of solitude are
enough – in the bath, or to fill
that gap between the Sunday papers and lunch.


## Mornings After


The surface dreams are easily remembered:
I wake most often with a comforting sense
of having seen a pleasantly odd film –
nothing too outlandish or too intense;

of having, perhaps, befriended animals,
made love, swum the Channel, flown in the air
without wings, visited Tibet or Chile:
simple childish stuff. Or else the rare

recurrent horror makes its call upon me:
I dream one of my sons is lost or dead,
or that I am trapped in a tunnel underground;
but my scream is enough to recall me to my bed.

Sometimes, indeed, I congratulate myself
on the nice precision of my observation:
on having seen so vividly a certain
colour; having felt the sharp sensation

of cold water on my hands; the exact taste
of wine or peppermints. I take a pride
in finding all my senses operative
even in sleep. So, with nothing to hide,

I amble through my latest entertainment
again, in the bath or going to work,
idly amused at what the night has offered;
unless this is a day when a sick jerk

recalls to me a sudden different vision:
I see myself inspecting the vast slit
of a sagging whore; making love with a hunchbacked
hermaphrodite; eating worms or shit;

or rapt upon necrophily or incest.
And whatever loathsome images I see
are just as vivid as the pleasant others.
I flush and shudder: my God, was that me?

Did I invent so ludicrously revolting
a scene? And if so, how could I forget
until this instant? And why now remember?
Furthermore (and more disturbing yet)

are all my other forgotten dreams like these?
Do I, for hours of my innocent nights,
wallow content and charmed through verminous muck,
rollick in the embraces of such frights?

And are the comic or harmless fantasies
I wake with merely a deceiving guard,
as one might put a Hans Andersen cover
on a volume of the writings of De Sade?

Enough, enough. Bring back those easy pictures,
Tibet or antelopes, a seemly lover,
or even the black tunnel. For the rest,
I do not care to know. Replace the cover.

# Gas

### 1

You recognise a body by its blemishes:
moles and birthmarks, scars, tattoos, oddly formed earlobes.
The present examination must be managed
in darkness, and by touch alone. That should suffice.
Starting at the head, then, there is a small hairless
scar on the left eyebrow; the bridge of the nose flat;
crowded lower teeth, and a chipped upper canine
(the lips part to let my fingers explore); a mole
on the right side of the neck.
                              No need to go on:
I know it all. But as I draw away, a hand
grips mine: a hand whose thumb bends back as mine does, whose
third finger bears the torn nail I broke in the door
last Thursday; and I feel these fingers check the scar
on my knuckle, measure my wrist's circumference,
move on gently exploring towards my elbow...

### 2

It was gas, we think.
Insects and reptiles survived it
and most of the birds;
also the larger mammals – grown
cattle, a few sheep,
horses, the landlord's Alsatian
(I shall miss the cats)
and, in this village, about a
fifth of the people.
It culled scientifically
within a fixed range,
sparing the insignificant
and the chosen strong.
It let us sleep for fourteen hours
and wake, not caring
whether we woke or not, in a
soft antiseptic
silence. There was a faint odour
of furniture-wax.
We know now, of course, more or less
what happened, but then
it was rather puzzling: to wake
from a thick dark sleep
lying on the carpeted floor

in the saloon bar
of the Coach and Horses; to sense
others lying near,
very still; and nearest to me
this new second self.


   3

I had one history until today:
now I shall have two.
No matter how nicely she may contrive
to do what I do
there are two hearts now for our identical
blood to pass through.

Nothing can change her. Whether she walks by my side
like a silly twin
or dyes her hair, adopts a new accent,
disguises her skin
with make-up and suntan, she cannot alter
the creature within.

She sees with my imperfect vision, she wears
my fingerprints; she is made
from me. If she should break the bones I gave her,
if disease should invade
her replicas of my limbs and organs,
which of us is betrayed?


   4

How was she torn out of me? Was it the
urgent wrench of birth, a matter of hard
breathless shoving (but there is no blood) or
Eve from Adam's rib, quick and surgical
(but there is no scar) or did I burgeon
with fleshy buds along my limbs, growing
a new substance from that gas I drank in,
to double myself? Did I perform the
amoeba's trick of separating into
two loose amorphous halves, a heart in each?
Or was my skin slipped off like the skin of
a peanut, to reveal two neat sections,
face to face and identical, within?
Yes, we had better say it was like this:
for if it was birth, which was the mother?
Since both have equal rights to our past, she
might justly claim to have created me.

5

It is the sixth day
now, and nothing much has happened.
Those of us who are
double (all the living ones) go
about our business.
The two Mrs Hudsons bake bread
in the pub kitchen
and contrive meals from what is left –
few shops are open.
The two Patricks serve in the bar
(Bill Hudson is dead).
I and my new sister stay here –
it seems easiest –
and help with the housework; sometimes
we go for walks, or
play darts or chess, finding ourselves
not as evenly
matched as we might have expected:
our capacity
is equal, but our moods vary.
These things occupy
the nights – none of us needs sleep now.
Only the dead sleep
laid out in all the beds upstairs.
They do not decay,
(some effect of the gas) and this
seemed a practical
and not irreverent means of
dealing with them. My
dead friend from London
and a housemaid from the hotel
lie in the bedroom
where we two go to change our clothes.
This evening when we
had done our hair before dinner
we combed and arranged
theirs too.

**6**

Saturday night in the bar; eight couples
fill it well enough: twin schoolteachers, two
of the young man from the garage, four girls
from the shop next door, some lads from the farms.
These woodenly try to chat up the girls,
but without heart. There is no sex now, when
each has his undeniable partner,
and no eyes or hands for any other.
Division, not union, is the way we
must reproduce now. Nor can one think with
desire or even curiosity
of one's identical other. How lust
for what is utterly familiar?
How place an auto-erotic hand on
a thigh which matches one's own? So we chat
about local events: the twin calves born,
it seems, on every farm; the corpse
in a well, and the water quite unspoiled;
the Post Office reopened, but with no
telephone links to places further than
the next town – just as there are no programmes
on television or radio, and
the single newspaper that we have seen
(a local one) contained only poems.
No one cares much for communication
outside this circle. I am forgetting
my work in London, my old concerns (we
laugh about the unpaid rent, the office
unmanned, the overdue library books).
They did a good job, whoever they were.


**7**

Two patterns of leaves above me: laurel
rather low, on my right,
and high on my left sycamore; a sky
pale grey: dawn or twilight.

Dew on my face, and on the gravel path
on which I am lying.
That scent of wax in the air, and a few
birds beginning to sing.

My mind is hazed by a long sleep – the first
for days. But I can tell
how it has been: the gas caught us walking
on this path, and we fell.

I feel a crystal, carolling lightness.
Beside me I can see
my newest self. It has happened again:
division, more of me.

Four, perhaps? We two stand up together,
dazed, euphoric, and go
to seek out our matching others, knowing
that they should be two, now.

My partner had been walking, I recall,
a little way ahead.
We find her. But there is only one. I
look upon myself, dead.


8

This is becoming ridiculous:
the gas visits us regularly,
dealing out death or duplication.
I am eight people now – and four dead
(these propped up against the trees in the
gardens, by the gravel walk). We eight
have inherited the pub, and shall,
if we continue to display our
qualities of durability,
inherit the village, God help us.
I see my image everywhere –
feeding the hens, hoeing the spinach,
peeling the potatoes, devising
a clever dish with cabbage and eggs.
I am responsible with and for
all. If B (we go by letters now)
forgets to light the fire, I likewise
have forgotten. If C breaks a cup
we all broke it. I am eight people,
a kind of octopus or spider,
and I cannot say it pleases me.
Sitting through our long sleepless nights, we
no longer play chess or poker (eight
identical hands, in which only

the cards are different). Now, instead,
we plan our death. Not quite suicide,
but a childish game: when the gas comes
(we can predict the time within a
margin of two days) we shall take care
to be in dangerous places. I can
see us all, wading in the river
for hours, taking long baths, finding
ladders and climbing to paint windows
on the third storey. It will be fun –
something, at last, to entertain us.


### 9

Winter. The village is silent –
no lights in the windows, and
a corpse in every snowdrift.
The electricity failed
months ago. We have chopped down half
the orchard for firewood,
and live on the apples we picked
in autumn. (That was a fine
harvest-day: three of us fell down
from high trees when the gas came.)
One way and another, in fact,
we are reduced now to two –
it can never be one alone,
for the survivor always
wakes with a twin.
                              We have great hopes
of the snow. At this moment
she is standing outside in it
like Socrates. We work shifts,
two hours each. But this evening
when gas-time will be closer
we are going to take blankets
and make up beds in the snow –
as if we were still capable
of sleep. And indeed, it may
come to us there: our only sleep.

**10**

Come, gentle gas

I lie and look at the night.
The stars look normal enough –
it has nothing to do with them –
and no new satellite
or comet has shown itself.
There is nothing up there to blame.

Come from wherever

She is quiet by my side.
I cannot see her breath
in the frost-purified air.
I would say she had died
if so natural a death
were possible now, here.

Come with what death there is

You have killed almost a score
of the bodies you made
from my basic design.
I offer you two more.
Let the mould be destroyed:
it is no longer mine.

Come, then, secret scented double-dealing gas.
We are cold: come and warm us.
We are tired: come and lull us.
Complete us.
Come. Please.

# THE SCENIC ROUTE

(1974)

# The Bullaun

'Drink water from the hollow in the stone…'
This was it, then – the cure for madness:
a rock with two round cavities, filled with rain;
a thing I'd read about once, and needed then,
but since forgotten. I didn't expect it here –
not having read the guidebook;
not having planned, even, to be in Antrim.
'There's a round tower, isn't there?' I'd asked.
The friendly woman in the post office
gave me directions: 'Up there past the station,
keep left, on a way further – it's a fair bit –
and have you been to Lough Neagh yet?' I walked –
it wasn't more than a mile – to the stone phallus
rising above its fuzz of beech trees
in the municipal gardens. And beside it,
this. I circled around them,
backing away over wet grass and beechmast,
aiming the camera (since I had it with me,
since I was playing tourist this afternoon)
and saw two little boys pelting across.
'Take our photo! Take our photo! Please!'
We talked it over for a bit –
how I couldn't produce one then and there;
but could I send it to them with the postman?
Well, could they give me their addresses?
Kevin Tierney and Declan McCallion,
Tobergill Gardens. I wrote, they stood and smiled,
I clicked, and waved goodbye, and went.
Two miles away, an hour later,
heading dutifully through the damp golf-course
to Lough Neagh, I thought about the rock,
wanting it. Not for my own salvation;
hardly at all for me: for sick Belfast,
for the gunmen and the slogan-writers,
for the poor crazy girl I met in the station,
for Kevin and Declan, who would soon mistrust
all camera-carrying strangers. But of course
the thing's already theirs: a monument,
a functionless, archaic, pitted stone
and a few mouthfuls of black rainwater.

# Please Identify Yourself

British, more or less; Anglican, of a kind.
In Cookstown I dodge the less urgent question
when a friendly Ulsterbus driver raises it;
'You're not a Moneymore girl yourself?' he asks,
deadpan. I make a cowardly retrogression,
slip ten years back. 'No, I'm from New Zealand.'
'Are you now? Well, that's a coincidence:
the priest at Moneymore's a New Zealander.'
And there's the second question, unspoken.
Unanswered.
                    I go to Moneymore
anonymously, and stare at all three churches.

In Belfast, though, where sides have to be taken,
I stop compromising – not that you'd guess,
seeing me hatless there among the hatted,
neutral voyeur among the shining faces
in the glossy Martyrs' Memorial Free Church.
The man himself is cheerleader in the pulpit
for crusader choruses: we're laved in blood,
marshalled in ranks. I chant the nursery tunes
and mentally cross myself. You can't stir me
with evangelistic hymns, Dr Paisley:
I know them. Nor with your computer-planned
sermon – Babylon, Revelation, whispers
of popery, slams at the IRA, more blood.
I scrawl incredulous notes under my hymnbook
and burn with Catholicism.
                    Later
hacking along the Lower Falls Road
against a gale, in my clerical black coat,
I meet a bright gust of tinselly children
in beads and lipstick and their mothers' dresses
for Hallowe'en; who chatter and surround me.
Over-reacting once again (a custom
of the country, not mine alone) I give them
all my loose change for their rattling tin
and my blessing – little enough. But now
to my tough Presbyterian ancestors,
Brooks and Hamilton, lying in the graves
I couldn't find at Moneymore and Cookstown
among so many unlabelled bones, I say:
I embrace you also, my dears.

# Richey

My great-grandfather Richey Brooks
began in mud: at Moneymore;
'a place of mud and nothing else'
he called it (not the way it looks,
but what lies under those green hills?)
Emigrated in '74;
ended in Drury: mud again –
slipped in the duck-run at ninety-three
(wouldn't give up keeping poultry,
always had to farm something).
Caught pneumonia; died saying
'Do you remember Martha Hamilton
of the Oritor Road?' – still courting
the same girl in his mind. And she
lived after him, fierce widow,
in their daughter's house; watched the plum tree –
the gnarled, sappy branches, the yellow
fruit. Ways of living and dying.

# The Voyage Out

The weekly dietary scale
per adult: pork and Indian beef,
three pounds together; one of sugar,
two of potatoes, three and a half
of flour; a gill of vinegar;
salt, pepper, a pint of oatmeal;
coffee, two ounces, likewise tea;
six of butter, suet, treacle,
and, in the tropics, of lime juice;
grudging grants of mustard and pickle;
split peas, raisins, currants, rice,
and half a pound of biscuit a day.
A diet for the young and fit:
monotonous, but not starvation –
and Martha traded half her ration
for extra lime juice from the crew.
Their quarters, also, adequate.
So not the middle passage; no.

But not a pleasure cruise, either.
A hundred days of travelling steerage
under capricious canvas; Martha
newly pregnant, struggling to manage
the first four (Tom, Eliza, Joe,
Annie); to keep them cool and clean
from a two-gallon can of water;
to calm their sleeping; to stay awake,
so heavy, herself; to protect the daughter
she rocked unborn in the swaying hammock
below her ribs (who would be Jane).
True, the family was together.
But who could envy Martha? Sick
with salt meat; thirsty; and gazing on
a sky huge as the whole Atlantic,
storm-waves like Slieve Gallion,
and no more Ireland than went with her.


## Train from the Hook of Holland


Not pill-boxes, exactly: blocks
of concrete, octagonal, serrated –
house-sized fancy buttons, roofed
with green turf. 'Hitler's Atlantic wall'
says the man in the corner seat.
On the other side of the train
lambs running, and, yes, a canal.
Then the low sun through a sea-haze
neon-red over – Maassluis, is it?
Some things, once you've got them,
are difficult to get rid of.
But we are happy, going somewhere.

# Nelia

She writes to me from a stony island
where they understand none of her languages.
Time has slipped out of its cogwheel:
she walks looking at plants and insects,
thinking without words, forgetting her home
and her work and her callous, temporary young lover.
Her children play like cicadas among the hills
and are safe. She cooks when they are hungry,
sleeps at will, wakes and runs to the sea.
I remember exactly the colour of her daughter's eyes –
glass-green; and the boy's light blue against his tan;
hers less clearly. But I see them now
as blue-black, reflecting an inky sky –
pure, without motes or atmosphere – that extends
uninterrupted from her to the still sun.

# Moa Point

At Moa Point that afternoon
two biologists were searching rockpools
for specimens. It was low tide.
I watched. They rolled away a stone,
fossicked in wet weed, described things
rather self-consciously to each other.
Then one of them put into my hands
a cold heavy jelly: my first sea-slug.
I peered gratefully down at it,
turned it over – did nothing, surely?
for them to laugh at. 'See that?'
said the one with freckles (they were both quite young)
'it doesn't seem to worry her.'
'Oh, well,' said the other 'these local kids…'
I kept my eyes down for a moment
in solemn, scientific study;
then said in my recently-acquired
almost local accent 'Thank you.'
And firmly but gently (a vet with a kitten)
handed it back.

## Briddes

'Briddes' he used to call them,
out of Chaucer – those cool
early-morning creatures
who tinkled in the elm trees.
Briddes talked us awake
and punctuated our childish
medieval loving.
All other birds were birds.


## The Famous Traitor

His jailer trod on a rose-petal.
There were others on the stone floor.
His desk tidy; some lines in pencil,
the bible open.
                    Years before
he'd lived like a private soldier –
a bag of nuts and the milk ration
for long days' marches. And under
the uniform a mathematician.
Puzzle-maker. After power:
which he got, this pastor's son
turned agnostic.
                    The nature
of his 'new kind of treason',
his links with the Nazi high command,
the deals, the sense of mission,
are well-documented; and
beyond every explanation.

He died 'with dignity' some said;
some that he had to wait an hour,
died shivering in the bitter cold.
It looked like fear. It was fear:
or it was not. And he did,
or did not, shake hands before
that moment with the firing-squad.
Authorities let us down here.

His final audience, the 'crowd
of notables', might as well
have been, as he was, blindfold.
We are left with the empty cell
like a film-set; the table
where the man of action/dreamer
made notes on his father's bible
in a litter of roses. Enter
his faithful jailer, to record
just this. The rest remains obscure
like all that made a dictionary word
of his name; like what he did it for.


## Script


'Wet the tea, Jinny, the men are back:
I can hear them out there, talking, with the horses,'
my mother's grandmother said. They both heard it,
she and her daughter – the wagon bumpily halted,
a rattle of harness, two familiar voices
in sentences to be identified later
and quoted endlessly. But the tea was cold
when the men came in. They'd been six miles away,
pausing to rest on Manurewa Hill
in a grove of trees – whence 'Fetch the nosebags, Dickie'
came clearly over. A freak wind, maybe:
soundwaves carrying, their words lifted up
and dropped on Drury. Eighty years ago,
long before the wireless was invented,
Grandma told us. It made a good story:
baffling. But then, so was the real thing –
radio.
            My father understood it.
Out on the bush farm at Te Rau a Moa
as a teenager he patiently constructed
little fiddly devices, sat for hours
every day adjusting a cat's whisker,
filtering morse through headphones. Later came
loudspeakers, and the whole family could gather
to hear the creaky music of 1YA.
So my father's people were technicians, is that it?

66

And my mother's were communicators, yes? –
Who worked as a barber in the evenings
for the talking's sake? Who became a teacher –
and who was in love with tractors? No prizes.
Don't classify. Leave the air-waves open.

We each extract what we most need. My sons
rig out their rooms with stereo equipment.
I walk dozily through the house
in the mornings with a neat black box,
audible newspaper, time-keeper and saver,
sufficient for days like that.
                              On days like this
I sit in my own high borrowed grove
and let the leafy air clear my mind
for reception. The slow pigeon-flight,
the scraped-wire pipping of some bird,
the loamy scent, offer themselves to me
as little presents, part of an exchange
to be continued and continually
(is this a rondo? that professor asked)
perpetuated. It is not like music,
though the effects can strike as music does:
it is more like agriculture, a nourishing
of the growth-mechanisms, a taking-in
of food for what will flower and seed and sprout.

On a path in the wood two white-haired women
are marching arm in arm, singing a hymn.
A girl stops me to ask where I bought my sandals.
I say 'In Italy, I think' and we laugh.
I am astonished several times a day.
When I get home I shall make tea or coffee
for whoever is there, talk and listen to talk,
share food and living-space. There will always
be time to reassemble the frail components
of this afternoon, to winnow the scattered sounds
dropped into my range, and rescue from them
a seed-hoard for transmission. There will be
always the taking-in and the sending-out.

# In Memoriam: James K. Baxter

Dear Jim, I'm using a Shakespearian form
to write you what I'll call a farewell letter.
Rhyming iambics have become the norm
for verse epistles, and I'm no trendsetter.
Perhaps you'll think it's going back a bit,
but as a craftsman you'll approve of it.

What better model have we, after all?
Dylan the Welshman, long your youthful passion,
doesn't quite do now, and the dying fall
of Eliot was never in your fashion.
Of North Americans the one you'd favour
is Lowell. But his salt has the wrong savour:

our ocean's called Pacific, not Atlantic –
which doesn't mean to say Neruda meets
the case. As for the classically romantic –
well, maybe it was easier for Keats:
I'd write with more conviction about death
if it were clutching at my every breath.

And now we've come to it. The subject's out:
the ineluctable, the all-pervasive.
Your death is what this letter's all about;
and if so far I've seemed a bit evasive
it's not from cowardice or phoney tact –
it's simply that I can't believe the fact.

I'd put you, with New Zealand, in cold storage
to wait for my return (should I so choose).
News of destruction can't delete an image:
what isn't seen to go, one doesn't lose.
The bulldozed streets, the buildings they've torn down
remain untouched until I'm back in town.

And so with you, framed in that sepia vision
a hemisphere away from me, and half
the twenty years I've known you. Such division
converts a face into a photograph:
a little blurred perhaps, the outlines dim,
but fixed, enduring, permanently Jim.

I saw you first when I was seventeen,
a word-struck student, ripe for dazzling. You
held unassuming court in the canteen –
the famous poet in the coffee-queue.
I watched with awe. But soon, as spheres are apt
to do in Wellington, ours overlapped.

I married, you might say, into the art.
You were my husband's friend; you'd wander in
on your way home from teaching, at the start,
for literary shop-talk over gin.
And then those fabled parties of one's youth:
home-brew and hot-lines to poetic truth.

Later the drinks were tea and lemonade,
the visits family ones, the talk less vatic;
and later still, down south, after I'd made
my getaway, came idiosyncratic
letters, your generous comments on my verse,
and poems of your own. But why rehearse

matters which you, acute observer, wise
recorder, don't forget? And now I falter,
knowing your present case: those tolerant eyes
will register no more. But I can't alter
this message to a dirge; the public attitude
isn't my style: I write in simple gratitude.

To think of elegies is to recall
several of yours. I find, when I look through
your varied, eloquent poems, nearly all
frosted with hints at death. What can I do
now, when it has become your own condition,
but praise all that you gave to the tradition?


## St John's School


When I went back the school was rather small
but not unexpectedly or oddly so.
I peered in at the windows of the hall
where we sang *O God Our Help* thirty years ago
for D-Day, the Normandy landings. It was all
as I'd pictured it. Outside, they'd cut the row

of dusty laurels, laid a lawn instead,
and the prefab classroom at the end was new;
but there were the lavatories, there was the shed
where we sat on rainy days with nothing to do,
giggling; and the beech trees overhead
whose fallen husks we used to riffle through

for triangular nuts. Yes, all as it should be –
no false images to negotiate,
no shocks. I wandered off contentedly
across the playground, out through the north gate,
down the still knee-straining slope, to see
what sprang up suddenly across the street:

the church, that had hardly existed in my past,
that had lurked behind a tree or two, unknown –
and uncensorious of me as I chased
squirrels over the graves – the church had grown:
high on its huge mound it soared, vast;
and God glared out from behind a tombstone.


## Pupation


Books, music, the garden, cats:
I have cocooned myself
in solitude, fatly silken.
Settled?
          I flatter myself.
Things buzz under my ribs;
there are ticklings, dim blunderings.
Ichneumon flies have got in.


## The Drought Breaks


That wet gravelly sound is rain.
Soil that was bumpy and crumbled
flattens under it, somewhere;
splatters into mud. Spiked grass
grows soft with it and bends like hair.
You lean over me, smiling at last.

# Kilpeck

We are dried and brittle this morning,
fragile with continence, quiet.
You have brought me to see a church.
I stare at a Norman arch in red sandstone
carved like a Mayan temple-gate;
at serpents writhing up the doorposts
and squat saints with South-American features
who stare back over our heads
from a panel of beasts and fishes.
The gargoyles jutting from under the eaves
are the colour of newborn children.

Last night you asked me
if poetry was the most important thing.

We walk on around the building
craning our heads back to look up
at lions, griffins, fat-faced bears.
The Victorians broke some of these figures
as being too obscene for a church;
but they missed the Whore of Kilpeck.
She leans out under the roof
holding her pink stony cleft agape
with her ancient little hands.
There was always witchcraft here, you say.

The sheep-track up to the fragments
of castle-wall is fringed with bright bushes.
We clamber awkwardly, separate.
Hawthorn and dog-rose offer hips and haws,
orange and crimson capsules, pretending
harvest. I taste a blackberry.
The soil here is coloured like brick-dust,
like the warm sandstone. A fruitful county.
We regard it uneasily.

There is little left to say
after all the talk we had last night
instead of going to bed –
fearful for our originality,
avoiding the sweet obvious act
as if it were the only kind of indulgence.

Silly perhaps.
                    We have our reward.
We are languorous now, heavy
with whatever we were conserving,
carrying each a delicate burden
of choices made or about to be made.
Words whisper hopefully in our heads.

Slithering down the track we hold hands
to keep a necessary balance.
The gargoyles extend their feral faces,
rosy, less lined than ours.
We are wearing out our identities.


## Feverish


Only a slight fever:
I was not quite out of my mind;
enough to forget my name
and the number and sex of my children
(while clinging to their existence –
three daughters, could it be?)
but not to forget my language
with *Words for Music Perhaps*,
Crazy Jane and the bishop,
galloping through my head.
As for my body, not
quite out of that either:
curled in an S-bend somewhere,
conscious of knees and skull
pressing against a wall
(if I was on my side)
or against a heavy lid
(if I was on my back);
or I could have been face downward
kneeling crouched on a raft,
castaway animal, drifting;
or shrivelled over a desk
head down asleep on it
like Harold, our wasted Orion,
who slept on the bare sand
all those nights in the desert

lightly, head on his briefcase;
who carried the new Peace
to chief after chief, winning
their difficult signatures
by wit and a cool head
under fire and public school charm;
who has now forgotten his Arabic
and the names of his brother's children
and what he did last week;
dozes over an ashtray
or shuffles through *Who Was Who*.
Crazy Jane I can take –
the withered breasts that she flaunted,
her fierce remembering tongue;
but spare me his forgetting.
Age is a sad fever.


## Folie à Deux


They call it pica,
this ranging after alien tastes:
acorns (a good fresh country food,
better than I'd remembered)
that morning in the wood,

and moonlit roses –
perfumed lettuce, rather unpleasant:
we rinsed them from our teeth with wine.
It seems a shared perversion,
not just a kink of mine –

you were the one
who nibbled the chrysanthemums.
All right: we are avoiding something.
Tonight you are here early.
We seem to lack nothing.

We are alone,
quiet, unhurried. The whisky has
a smoky tang, like dark chocolate.
You speak of ceremony, of
something to celebrate.

I hear the church bells
and suddenly fear blasphemy,
even name it. The word's unusual
between us. But you don't laugh.
We postpone our ritual

and act another:
sit face to face across a table,
talk about places we have known
and friends who are still alive
and poems (not our own).

It works. We are altered
from that fey couple who talked out
fountains of images, a spray
of loves, deaths, dramas, jokes:
their histories; who lay

manic with words,
fingers twined in each other's hair
(no closer) wasting nights and hours;
who chewed, as dry placebos,
those bitter seeds and flowers.

It is the moment.
We rise, and touch at last. And now
without pretence or argument,
fasting, and in our right minds,
go to our sacrament.


## Acris Hiems


A letter from that pale city
I escaped from ten years ago
and no good news.
I carry it with me
devising comfortable answers
(the sickness, shall I say?
is not peculiarly yours),
as I walk along Beech Drive,
Church Vale, Ringwood Avenue
at eleven on a Tuesday morning
going nowhere.

A bony day, an invisible wind,
the sky white as an ambulance,
and no one in sight.
Friend, I will say in my letter –
since you call me a friend still,
whatever I have been – forgive me.
Rounding the next corner
I see a van that crawls along
beside the birch-trunks and pink pavements.
A handbell rings from the driver's window:
he has paraffin for sale
and ought to do good business
now that we have power-cuts.
But the painted doors do not open.
The wind in the ornamental hedges
rustles. Nobody comes.
The bell rings. The houses listen.
Bring out your dead.


## December Morning


I raise the blind and sit by the window
dry-mouthed, waiting for light.
One needs a modest goal,
something safely attainable.
An hour before sunrise
(due at seven fifty-three)
I go out into the cold new morning
for a proper view of that performance;
walk greedily towards the heath
gulping the blanched air
and come in good time to Kenwood.
They have just opened the gates.
There is a kind of world here, too:
on the grassy slopes above the lake
in the white early Sunday
I see with something like affection
people I do not know
walking their unlovable dogs.

## Showcase

Looking through the glass showcase
right into the glass of the shelf,
your eye level with it, not
swerving above it or below,
you see neither the reflected image
nor the object itself.

There is only a swimming horizon,
a watery prison for the sight,
acres of shadowy green jelly,
and no way yet to know
what they support, what stands
in the carefully-angled light.

You take a breath, raise your head,
and see whether the case reveals
Dutch goblet, carved reliquary,
the pope's elaborately-petalled rose
of gold-leaf, or the bronze Cretan
balanced on his neat heels,

and you look, drowning or perhaps
rescued from drowning; and your eyes close.

## Over the Edge

All my dead people
seeping through the riverbank where they are buried
colouring the stream pale brown
are why I swim in the river,
feeling now rather closer to them
than when the water was clear,
when I could walk barefoot on the gravel
seeing only the flicker of minnows
possessing nothing but balance.

# The Net

She keeps the memory-game
as a charm against falling in love
and each night she climbs out of the same window
into the same garden with the arch for roses –
no roses, though; and the white snake dead too;
nothing but evergreen shrubs, and grass, and water,
and the wire trellis that will trap her in the end.


# An Illustration to Dante

Here are Paolo and Francesca
whirled around in the circle of Hell
clipped serenely together
her dead face raised against his.
I can feel the pressure of his arms
like yours about me, locking.

They float in a sea of whitish blobs –
fire, is it? It could have been
hail, said Ruskin, but Rossetti
'didn't know how to do hail'.
Well, he could do tenderness.
My spine trickles with little white flames.


# Tokens

The sheets have been laundered clean
of our joint essence – a compound,
not a mixture; but here are still

your forgotten pipe and tobacco,
your books open on my table,
your voice speaking in my poems.

# Naxal

The concrete road from the palace to the cinema
bruises the feet. At the Chinese Embassy
I turn past high new walls on to padded mud.
A road is intended – men with trowels and baskets
work on it daily, dreamy Nepali girls
tilt little pots of water on to cement –
but it's gentle walking now. It leads 'inside'.
The tall pine at the end – still notable
though it lost its lingam top for winter firewood –
begins the village: a couple of streets, a temple,
an open space with the pond and the peepul tree,
rows of brick houses, little businesses
proceeding under their doll's-house-level beams;
rice being pounded, charcoal fires in pots,
rickshaws for people like me who don't want them.
The children wave and call 'Bye-bye! Paisa?'
holding out their perfect hands for my coins.
These houses may be eighteenth-century:
I covet their fretted lattice window-frames
and stare slightly too long into back rooms.
There are no screens at the carved windows, no filters
for the water they splash and drink at the common pump;
and no mosquitoes now, in the early spring.
But finally, stepping over the warm threshold
of the temple courtyard, I feel a tentative itch;
passing the scummy tank, a little sickness;
touching an infant's head, a little pain.

# Bodnath

I have made my pilgrimage a day early:
Ash Wednesday is tomorrow; this week is Losar.
Pacing clockwise around the chaitya
I twirl the prayerwheels, my foreign fingers
polishing their bronze by a fraction more.
The courtyard is crowded with Tibetans,
incredibly jewelled and furred and hatted –
colour-plates from the National Geographic.
The beggar-woman with her monstrous leg
and the snuffling children are genuine too.
I toss them paisa; then go to spend
thirty rupees on a turquoise-studded
silver spoon for the Watkins' baby.

High on his whitewashed mound, Lord Buddha
overlooks the blossom of kite-tails
fluttering from his solid neck.
Om Mani Padme Hum.
His four painted square faces
turn twelve coloured eyes on the globe.
In the shrine below I see him again:
dim bronze, made of curves and surfaces,
shadowed, vulnerable, retiring.
Filmy scarves of white muslin
veil him; rice-grains lie at his feet;
in copper bowls arranged before him
smouldering incense crumbles to ash.

## External Service

Already I know my way around the bazaar,
can use half a dozen words of basic Nepali,
and recognise several incarnations of Shiva.
If I stay here much longer I shall learn to identify
more trees besides those in our compound,
other birds than the rock-dove and the crow.
That plink-plink rhythm in the distance is a rice-mill.
The cannon is fired at noon, or to mark a death –
an echoing gesture. Now on the foreign news
I hear that the serious thunder-makers from Ireland
have crossed the channel. A pall of thick black smoke,
says the tidy English voice, hangs over London.
Here the sky is crystal. It is time to go.

## Flying Back

They give us moistened BOAC towels
and I scrub my forehead. Red powder
for Holi: a trace of Delhi, an assault
met there in the wild streets this morning.
Without compunction I obliterate it –
India's not my country, let it go.
But crumpling the vermilion-stained napkin
(I shan't read it: some priest may do that)
I think of the stone foreheads in their hundreds:
Ganesh and Hanuman, who made me smile,
and Vishnu, and the four faces of Buddha,
reddened with genuine devotions;
and of the wooden cleft in a twisted tree
which I saw a beggar-woman sign scarlet
before she pressed her face down on to it;
and here's Nepal again. Sacred places
don't travel. The gods are stronger at home.
But if my tentative western brow may wear
this reluctant blush, these grains at the hair-roots,
I claim the right also to an image
as guardian; and choose winged Garuda.
His bland archaic countenance beams out
that serenity to which I journey.

# Near Creeslough

I am in a foreign country.
There are heron and cormorant on the lake.
Young men in T-shirts against an Atlantic gale
are wheeling gravel, renewing the paths
in a stone shell chalked with their own history:

something to fear and covet.
We are the only visitors.
Notices tell us in two old languages
(one mine) that this is Caisleán na dTúath,
Doe Castle. A castle for everyman.

It has ramparts, towers, a dungeon –
we step over gridded emptiness.
The floors have rotted away in seventy years;
the spiral stair endures, a little chipped,
after four hundred. Here is my phobia.

And for you, at the top of it,
yours: a wind-racked vacancy,
a savage drop, a view with no holds –
to which you climb; and if you do, I do:
going up, after all, is the lesser challenge.

The high ledge receives us.
We stand there half a minute longer
than honour and simple vanity require;
then I follow you down the stone gullet,
feet on the splintering treads, eyes inward,

and we step on springy grass
once again; there have been no lapses.
Now ravens ferrying food up to a nest
make their easy ascents. Pleased with our own
we stroll away to eat oranges in the car.

# Kilmacrenan

The hailstorm was in my head.
It drove us out into the blind lanes
to stumble over gravel and bog,
teeter on the skidding riverbank
together, stare down and consider.
But we drew back. When the real hail
began its pounding upon us
we were already half recovered.
Walking under that pouring icefall
hand in hand, towards lighted rooms,
we became patchworks of cold and hot,
glowing, streaming with water,
dissolving whatever dared to touch us.

# Glenshane

Abandoning all my principles
I travel by car with you for days,
eat meat from tins, drink pints of Guinness,
smoke too much, and now on this pass
higher than all our settled landscapes
feed salted peanuts into your mouth
as you drive at eighty miles an hour.

# THE INNER HARBOUR

(1979)

## Future Work

'Please send future work.'
— EDITOR'S NOTE ON A REJECTION SLIP

It is going to be a splendid summer.
The apple tree will be thick with golden russets
expanding weightily in the soft air.
I shall finish the brick wall beside the terrace
and plant out all the geranium cuttings.
Pinks and carnations will be everywhere.

She will come out to me in the garden,
her bare feet pale on the cut grass,
bringing jasmine tea and strawberries on a tray.
I shall be correcting the proofs of my novel
(third in a trilogy – simultaneous publication
in four continents); and my latest play

will be in production at the Aldwych
starring Glenda Jackson and Paul Scofield
with Olivier brilliant in a minor part.
I shall probably have finished my translations
of Persian creation myths and the Pre-Socratics
(drawing new parallels) and be ready to start

on Lucretius. But first I'll take a break
at the chess championships in Manila –
on present form, I'm fairly likely to win.
And poems? Yes, there will certainly be poems:
they sing in my head, they tingle along my nerves.
It is all magnificently about to begin.

# Our Trip to the Federation

We went to Malaya for an afternoon,
driving over the long dull roads
in Bill's Toyota, the two boys in the back.
It was rubber plantations mostly
and villages like all Asian villages,
brown with dust and wood, bright with marketing.

Before we had to turn back we stopped
at a Chinese roadside cemetery
and visited among the long grass
the complicated coloured graves,
patchwork semi-circles of painted stone:
one mustn't set a foot on the wrong bit.

Across the road were rubber trees again
and a kampong behind: we looked in
at thatched houses, flowering shrubs, melons,
unusual speckled poultry, and the usual
beautiful children. We observed
how the bark was slashed for rubber-tapping.

Does it sound like a geography lesson
or a dream? Rubber-seeds are mottled,
smooth, like nuts. I picked up three
and have smuggled them absent-mindedly
in and out of several countries.
Shall I plant them and see what grows?

## Mr Morrison

Goslings dive in the lake,
leaves dazzle on the trees;
on the warm grass two ducks are parked neatly
together like a pair of shoes.

A coot plays beaks with its chick;
children laugh and exclaim.
Mr Morrison saunters past, smiling at them,
humming a Sunday-school hymn.

He wonders about his mood,
irredeemably content:
he should worry more about poverty, oppression,
injustice; but he can't, he can't.

He is not too callous to care
but is satisfied in his work,
well-fed, well-housed, tolerably married,
and enjoying a walk in the park.

Then the sun sticks in the sky,
the tune sticks in his throat,
a burning hand with razors for fingernails
reaches inside his coat

and hotly claws at his heart.
He stands very quiet and still,
seeing if he dares to breathe just a fraction;
sweating; afraid he'll fall.

With stiff little wooden steps
he edges his way to a bench
and lowers his body with its secret fiery
tenant down, inch by inch.

He orders himself to be calm:
no doubt it will soon pass.
He resolves to smoke less, watch his cholesterol,
walk more, use the car less.

And it passes: he is released,
the stabbing fingers depart.
Tentatively at first, then easily,
he fills his lungs without hurt.

He is safe; and he is absolved:
it was not just pain, after all;
it enrolled him among the sufferers, allotted him
a stake in the world's ill.

Doors open inside his head;
once again he begins to hum:
he's been granted one small occasion for worry
and the promise of more to come.

## Things

There are worse things than having behaved foolishly in public.
There are worse things than these miniature betrayals,
committed or endured or suspected; there are worse things
than not being able to sleep for thinking about them.
It is 5 a.m. All the worse things come stalking in
and stand icily about the bed looking worse and worse and worse.

## A Way Out

The other option's to become a bird.
That's kindly done, to guess from how they sing,
decently independent of the word
as we are not; and how they use the air
to sail as we might soaring on a swing
higher and higher; but the rope's not there,

it's free fall upward, out into the sky;
or if the arc veer downward, then it's planned:
a bird can loiter, skimming just as high
as lets him supervise the hazel copse,
the turnip field, the orchard, and then land
on just the twig he's chosen. Down he drops

to feed, if so it be: a pretty killer,
a keen-eyed stomach weighted like a dart.
He feels no pity for the caterpillar,
that moistly munching hoop of innocent green.
It is such tender lapses twist the heart.
A bird's heart is a tight little red bean,

untwistable. His beak is made of bone,
his feet apparently of stainless wire;
his coat's impermeable; his nest's his own.
The clogging multiplicity of things
amongst which other creatures, battling, tire
can be evaded by a pair of wings.

The point is, most of it occurs below,
earthed at the levels of the grovelling wood
and gritty buildings. Up's the way to go.
If it's escapist, if it's like a dream
the dream's prolonged until it ends for good.
I see no disadvantage in the scheme.


## Prelude


Is it the long dry grass that is so erotic,
waving about us with hair-fine fronds of straw,
with feathery flourishes of seed, inviting us
to cling together, fall, roll into it
blind and gasping, smothered by stalks and hair,
pollen and each other's tongues on our hot faces?
Then imagine if the summer rain were to come,
heavy drops hissing through the warm air,
a sluice on our wet bodies, plastering us
with strands of delicious grass; a hum in our ears.

We walk a yard apart, talking
of literature and of botany.
We have known each other, remotely, for nineteen years.

# Accidental

We awakened facing each other
across the white counterpane.
I prefer to be alone in the mornings.
The waiter offered us
melon, papaya, orange juice or fresh raspberries.
We did not discuss it.

All those years of looking but not touching:
at most a kiss in a taxi.
And now this accident,
this blind unstoppable robot walk
into a conspiracy of our bodies.
Had we ruined the whole thing?

The waiter waited:
it was his business to appear composed.
Perhaps we should make it ours also?
We moved an inch or two closer together.
Our toes touched. We looked. We had decided.
Papaya then; and coffee and rolls. Of course.


# A Message

Discreet, not cryptic. I write to you from the garden
in tawny, provoking August; summer is just
on the turn. The lawn is hayseeds and grassy dust.

There are brilliant yellow daisies, though, and fuchsia
(you'll know why) and that mauve and silvery-grey
creeper under the apple tree where we lay.

There have been storms. The apples are few, but heavy,
heavy. And where blossom was, the tree
surges with bright pink flowers – the sweet pea

has taken it over again. Things operate
oddly here. Remember how I found
the buddleia dead, and cut it back to the ground?

That was in April. Now it's ten feet high:
thick straight branches – they've never been so strong –
leaves like a new species, half a yard long,

and spikes of flowers, airily late for their season
but gigantic. A mutation, is it? Well,
summers to come will test it. Let time tell.

Gardens are rife with sermon-fodder. I delve
among blossoming accidents for their designs
but make no statement. Read between these lines.


## Proposal for a Survey

Another poem about a Norfolk church,
a neolithic circle, Hadrian's Wall?
Histories and prehistories: indexes
and bibliographies can't list them all.
A map of Poets' England from the air
could show not only who and when but where.

Aerial photogrammetry's the thing,
using some form of infra-red technique.
Stones that have been so fervently described
surely retain some heat. They needn't speak:
the cunning camera ranging in its flight
will chart their higher temperatures as light.

We'll see the favoured regions all lit up –
the Thames a fiery vein, Cornwall a glow,
Tintagel like an incandescent stud,
most of East Anglia sparkling like Heathrow;
and Shropshire luminous among the best,
with Offa's Dyke in diamonds to the west.

The Lake District will be itself a lake
of patchy brilliance poured along the vales,
with somewhat lesser splashes to the east
across Northumbria and the Yorkshire dales.
Cities and churches, villages and lanes,
will gleam in sparks and streaks and radiant stains.

The lens, of course, will not discriminate
between the venerable and the new;
Stonehenge and Avebury may catch the eye
but Liverpool will have its aura too.
As well as Canterbury there'll be Leeds
and Hull criss-crossed with nets of glittering beads.

Nor will the cool machine be influenced
by literary fashion to reject
any on grounds of quality or taste:
intensity is all it will detect,
mapping in light, for better or for worse,
whatever has been written of in verse.

The dreariness of eighteenth-century odes
will not disqualify a crag, a park,
a country residence; nor will the rant
of satirists leave London in the dark.
All will shine forth. But limits there must be:
borders will not be crossed, nor will the sea.

Let Scotland, Wales and Ireland chart themselves,
as they'd prefer. For us, there's just one doubt:
that medieval England may be dimmed
by age, and all that's earlier blotted out.
X-rays might help. But surely ardent rhyme
will, as it's always claimed, outshine mere time?

By its own power the influence will rise
from sites and settlements deep underground
of those who sang about them while they stood.
Pale phosphorescent glimmers will be found
of epics chanted to pre-Roman tunes
and poems in, instead of about, runes.

# Fairy-tale

This is a story. Dear Clive
(a name unmet among my acquaintance)
you landed on my island: Mauritius
I'll call it – it was not unlike.
The Governor came to meet your plane.
I stood on the grass by the summerhouse.
It was dark, I think. And next morning
we walked in the ripples of the sea
watching the green and purple creatures
flashing in and out of the waves
about our ankles. Seabirds, were they?
Or air-fishes, a flying shoal
of sea-parrots, finned and feathered?
Even they were less of a marvel,
pretty things, than that you'd returned
after a year and such distraction
to walk with me on the splashy strand.


# At the Creative Writing Course

Slightly frightened of the bullocks
as we walk into their mud towards them
she arms herself by naming them for me:
'Friesian, Aberdeen, Devon, South Devon...'
A mixed herd. I was nervous too,
but no longer. 'Devon, Friesian, Aberdeen...'
the light young voice chants at them
faster as the long heavy heads
lift and lurch towards us. And pause,
turn away to let us pass. I am learning
to show confidence before large cattle.
She is learning to be a poet.

*Endings*

## The Ex-Queen Among the Astronomers

They serve revolving saucer eyes,
dishes of stars; they wait upon
huge lenses hung aloft to frame
the slow procession of the skies.

They calculate, adjust, record,
watch transits, measure distances.
They carry pocket telescopes
to spy through when they walk abroad.

Spectra possess their eyes; they face
upwards, alert for meteorites,
cherishing little glassy worlds:
receptacles for outer space.

But she, exile, expelled, ex-queen,
swishes among the men of science
waiting for cloudy skies, for nights
when constellations can't be seen.

She wears the rings he let her keep;
she walks as she was taught to walk
for his approval, years ago.
His bitter features taunt her sleep.

And so when these have laid aside
their telescopes, when lids are closed
between machine and sky, she seeks
terrestrial bodies to bestride.

She plucks this one or that among
the astronomers, and is become
his canopy, his occultation;
she sucks at earlobe, penis, tongue

mouthing the tubes of flesh; her hair
crackles, her eyes are comet-sparks.
She brings the distant briefly close
above his dreamy abstract stare.

## Off the Track

Our busy springtime has corrupted
into a green indolence of summer,
static, swollen, invisibly devoured.
Too many leaves have grown between us.
Almost without choosing I have turned
from wherever we were towards this thicket
It is not the refuge I had hoped for.
Walking away from you I walk
into a trailing mist of caterpillars:
they swing at my face, tinily suspended,
half-blinding; and my hands are smudged
with a syrup of crushed aphids.

You must be miles away by now
in open country, climbing steadily,
head down, looking for larks' eggs.


## Beaux Yeux

Arranging for my due ration of terror
involves me in such lunacies
as recently demanding to be shown
the broad blue ovals of your eyes.

Yes: quite as alarming as you'd promised,
those lapidary iris discs
level in your dark small face.
Still, for an hour or two I held them

until you laughed, replaced your tinted glasses,
switched accents once again
and went away, looking faintly uncertain
in the sunlight (but in charge, no doubt of it)

and leaving me this round baby sparrow
modelled in feather-coloured clay,
a small snug handful; hardly apt
unless in being cooler than a pebble.

# Send-off

Half an hour before my flight was called
he walked across the airport bar towards me
carrying what was left of our future
together: two drinks on a tray.

# In Focus

Inside my closed eyelids, printed out
from some dying braincell as I awakened,
was this close-up of granular earthy dust,
fragments of chaff and grit, a triangular
splinter of glass, a rusty metal washer
on rough concrete under a wooden step.

Not a memory. But the caption told me
I was at Grange Farm, seven years old,
in the back yard, kneeling outside the shed
with some obscure seven-year-old's motive,
seeing as once, I must believe, I saw:
sharply; concentrating as once I did.

Glad to be there again I relaxed the focus
(eyes still shut); let the whole scene open out
to the pump and separator under the porch,
the strolling chickens, the pear trees next to the yard,
the barn full of white cats, the loaded haycart,
the spinney... I saw it rolling on and on.

As it couldn't, of course. That I had faced
when I made my compulsive return visit
after more than twenty years. 'Your aunt's not well,'
said Uncle George – little and gnarled himself –
'You'll find she doesn't talk.' They'd sold the farm,
retired to Melton Mowbray with their daughter.

'Premature senility,' she whispered.
But we all went out together in the car
to see the old place, Auntie sitting
straight-backed, dignified, mute,
perhaps a little puzzled as we churned
through splattering clay lanes, between wet hedges

to Grange Farm again: to a square house,
small, bleak, and surrounded by mud;
to be greeted, shown to the parlour, given tea,
with Auntie's affliction gently signalled –
'Her mouth hurts.' Not my real aunt,
nor my real uncle. Both dead now.

I find it easiest to imagine dying
as like the gradual running down of a film,
the brain still flickering when the heart and blood
have halted, and the last few frames
lingering. Then where the projector jams
is where we go, or are, or are no longer.

If that comes anywhere near it, then I hope
that for those two an after-image glowed
in death of something better than mud and silence
or than my minute study of a patch of ground;
unless, like that for me, it spread before them
sunny ploughland, pastures, the scented orchard.


## Letter from Highgate Wood


Your 'wedge of stubborn particles':

that silver birch, thin as a bent flagpole,
drives up through elm and oak and hornbeam
to sky-level, catching the late sunlight.

There's woodsmoke, a stack of cut billets
from some thick trunk they've had to hack;
and of course a replacement programme under way –
saplings fenced off against marauders.

'We have seasons' your poem says;
and your letter tells me the black invader
has moved into the lymph; is not defeated.

'He's lucky to be still around,' said your friend –
himself still around, still travelling
after a near-axing as severe,
it yet may prove, as yours at present.

I have come here to think, not for comfort;
to confront these matters, to imagine
the proliferating ungentle cells.

But the place won't let me be fearful;
the green things work their usual trick –
'Choose life' – and I remember instead
our own most verdant season.

My dear, after more than a dozen years
light sings in the leaves of it still.


## Poem Ended by a Death


They will wash all my kisses and fingerprints off you
and my tearstains – I was more inclined to weep
in those wild-garlicky days – and our happier stains,
thin scales of papery silk... Fuck that for a cheap
opener; and false too – any such traces
you pumiced away yourself, those years ago
when you sent my letters back, in the week I married
that anecdotal ape. So start again. So:

They will remove the tubes and drips and dressings
which I censor from my dreams. They will, it is true,
wash you; and they will put you into a box.
After which whatever else they may do
won't matter. This is my laconic style.
You praised it, as I praised your intricate pearled
embroideries; these links laced us together,
plain and purl across the ribs of the world...

# Having No Mind for the Same Poem

Nor for the same conversation again and again.
But the power of meditation to cure an allergy,
that I will discuss
cross-legged on the lawn at evening
midges flittering, a tree beside us
none of us can name;
and rocks; a scent of syringa;
certain Japanese questions; the journey...

Nor for parody.

Nor, if we come to it, for the same letter:
'hard to believe... I remember best his laugh...
such a vigorous man...please tell...'
and running, almost running to stuff coins
into the box for cancer research.

The others.

Nor for the same hopeless prayer.

## Syringa

The syringa's out. That's nice for me:
all along Charing Cross Embankment
the sweet dragging scent reinventing
one of my childhood gardens.
Nice for the drunks and drop-outs too,
if they like it. I'm walking to work:
they'll be here all day under the blossom
with their cider and their British sherry
and their carrier-bags of secrets.
There's been a change in the population:
the ones I had names for – Fat Billy,
the Happy Couple, the Lady with the Dog –
have moved on or been moved off.
But it doesn't do to wonder:
staring hurts in two directions. Once
a tall man chased me here, and I ran
for no good reason: afraid, perhaps,
of turning into Mrs Toothless
with her ankle-socks and her pony-tailed skull
whose eyes avoided mine so many mornings.
And she's gone too. The place has been,
as whatever office will have termed it,
cleaned up. Except that it's not clean
and not really a place: a hesitation
between the traffic fumes and a fragrance,
where this evening I shall walk again.

*The Thing Itself*

## Dry Spell

It is not one thing, but more one thing than others:
the carved spoon broken in its case, a slate split on the roof,
dead leaves falling upon dead grass littered
with feathers, and the berries ripe too soon.

All of a piece and all in pieces, the dry mouth failing
to say it. I am sick with symbols.
Here is the thing itself: it is a drought.
I must learn it and live it drably through.

## Visited

This truth-telling is well enough
looking into the slaty eyes of the visitants
acknowledging the messages they bring

but they plod past so familiarly
mouldy faces droning about acceptance
that one almost looks for a real monster

spiny and gaping as the fine mad fish
in the corner of that old shipwreck painting
rearing its red gullet out of the foam.

# The Soho Hospital for Women

### 1

Strange room, from this angle:
white door open before me,
strange bed, mechanical hum, white lights.
There will be stranger rooms to come.

As I almost slept I saw the deep flower opening
and leaned over into it, gratefully.
It swimmingly closed in my face. I was not ready.
It was not death, it was acceptance.

\*

Our thin patient cat died purring,
her small triangular head tilted back,
the nurse's fingers caressing her throat,
my hand on her shrunken spine; the quick needle.

That was the second death by cancer.
The first is not for me to speak of.
It was telephone calls and brave letters
and a friend's hand bleeding under the coffin.

\*

Doctor, I am not afraid of a word.
But neither do I wish to embrace that visitor,
to engulf it as Hine-Nui-te-Po
engulfed Maui; that would be the way of it.

And she was the winner there: her womb crushed him.
Goddesses can do these things.
But I have admitted the gloved hands and the speculum
and must part my ordinary legs to the surgeon's knife.

### 2

Nellie has only one breast
ample enough to make several.
Her quilted dressing-gown softens
to semi-doubtful this imbalance
and there's no starched vanity
in our abundant ward-mother:
her silvery hair's in braids, her slippers
loll, her weathered smile holds true.
When she dresses up in her black

with her glittering marcasite brooch on
to go for the weekly radium treatment
she's the bright star of the taxi-party –
whatever may be growing under her ribs.

*

Doris hardly smokes in the ward –
and hardly eats more than a dreamy spoonful –
but the corridors and bathrooms
reek of her Players Number 10,
and the drug-trolley pauses
for long minutes by her bed.
Each week for the taxi-outing
she puts on her skirt again
and has to pin the slack waistband
more tightly over her scarlet sweater.
Her face, a white shadow through smoked glass,
lets Soho display itself unregarded.

*

Third in the car is Mrs Golding
who never smiles. And why should she?

3

The senior consultant on his rounds
murmurs in so subdued a voice
to the students marshalled behind
that they gather in, forming a cell,
a cluster, a rosette around him
as he stands at the foot of my bed
going through my notes with them,
half-audibly instructive, grave.

The slight ache as I strain forward
to listen still seems imagined.

Then he turns his practised smile on me:
'How are you this morning?' 'Fine,
very well, thank you.' I smile too.
And possibly all that murmurs within me
is the slow dissolving of stitches.

4

I am out in the supermarket choosing –
this very afternoon, this day –
picking up tomatoes, cheese, bread,

things I want and shall be using
to make myself a meal, while they
eat their stodgy suppers in bed:

Janet with her big freckled breasts,
her prim Scots voice, her one friend,
and never in hospital before,

who came in to have a few tests
and now can't see where they'll end;
and Coral in the bed by the door

who whimpered and gasped behind a screen
with nurses to and fro all night
and far too much of the day;

pallid, bewildered, nineteen.
And Mary, who will be all right
but gradually. And Alice, who may.

Whereas I stand almost intact,
giddy with freedom, not with pain.
I lift my light basket, observing

how little I needed in fact;
and move to the checkout, to the rain,
to the lights and the long street curving.


## Variations on a Theme of Horace

Clear is the man and of a cold life
who needn't fear the slings and arrows;
cold is the man, and perhaps the moorish bows
will avoid him and the wolf turn tail.

\*

Sitting in the crypt under bare arches
at a quite ordinary table with a neat cloth,
a glass of wine before him, 'I'm never sure,'
he said, 'that I'll wake up tomorrow morning.'

Upstairs musicians were stretching their bows
for a late quartet which would also save us from nothing.
This ex-church was bombed to rubble,
rebuilt. It is not of that he was thinking.

And policemen decorate the underground stations
to protect us from the impure of heart;
the traveller must learn to suspect his neighbour,
each man his own watchdog. Nor of that.

Of a certain high felicity, perhaps,
imagining its absence; of the chances.
(If echoes fall into the likeness of music
that, like symmetry, may be accidental.)

'Avoid archaism for its own sake –
viols, rebecks: what is important
is simply that the instruments should be able
to play the notes.' A hard-learnt compromise.

But using what we have while we have it
seems, at times, enough or more than enough.
And here were old and newer things for our pleasure –
the sweet curves of the arches; music to come.

Which this one set before him with his own death –
far from probably imminent, not soon likely –
ticking contrapuntally like a pace-maker
inside him. Were we, then, lighter, colder?

Had we ignored a central insistent theme?
Possibly even the birds aren't happy:
it may be that they twitter from rage or fear.
So many tones; one can't be sure of one's reading.

Just as one can't quite despise Horace
on whom the dreaded tree never did quite fall;
timid enjoyer that he was, he died
in due course of something or other. And meanwhile

sang of his Lalage in public measures,
enjoyed his farm and his dinners rather more,
had as much, no doubt, as any of us to lose.
And the black cypress stalks after us all.

# A Walk in the Snow

Neighbours lent her a tall feathery dog
to make her expedition seem natural.
She couldn't really fancy a walk alone,
drawn though she was to the shawled whiteness,
the flung drifts of wool. She was not a walker.
Her winter pleasures were in firelit rooms –
entertaining friends with inventive dishes
or with sherry, conversation, palm-reading:
'You've suffered,' she'd say. 'Of course, life is suffering...'
holding a wrist with her little puffy hand
older than her face. She was writing a novel.
But today there was the common smothered in snow,
blanked-out, white as meringue, the paths gone:
a few mounds of bracken spikily veiled
and the rest smooth succulence. They pocked it,
she and the dog; they wrote on it with their feet –
her suede boots, his bright flurrying paws.
It was their snow, and they took it.
                              That evening
the poltergeist, the switcher-on of lights
and conjuror with ashtrays, was absent.
The house lay mute. She hesitated a moment
at bedtime before the Valium bottle;
then, to be on the safe side, took her usual;
and swam into a deep snowy sleep
where a lodge (was it?) and men in fur hats,
and the galloping... and something about...


# A Day in October

*1.30 p.m.*
Outside the National Gallery
a man checks bags for bombs or weapons –
not thoroughly enough: he'd have missed
a tiny hand-grenade in my make-up purse,
a cigarette packet of gelignite.
I walk in gently to Room III
not to disturb them: Piero's angels,
serene and cheerful, whom surely nothing could frighten,
and St Michael in his red boots
armed against all comers.

Brave images. But under my heart
an explosive bubble of tenderness gathers
and I shiver before the chalky Christ:
what must we do to save
the white limbs, pale tree, trusting verticals?
Playing the old bargaining game
I juggle with prices, offer a finger
for this or that painting, a hand or an eye
for the room's contents. What for the whole building?
And shouldn't I jump aside if the bomb flew,
cowardly as instinct makes us?
'Goodbye' I tell the angels, just in case.

*4 p.m.*
It's a day for pictures:
this afternoon, in the course of duty,
I open a book of black-and-white photographs,
rather smudgy, the text quaintly translated
from the Japanese: Atomic Bomb Injuries.
All the familiar shots are here:
the shadow blast-printed on to a wall,
the seared or bloated faces of children.
I am managing not to react to them.
Then this soldier, who died from merely helping,
several slow weeks afterwards.
His body is a Scarfe cartoon –
skinny trunk, enormous toes and fingers,
joints huge with lymphatic nodes.
My throat swells with tears at last.
Almost I fall into that inheritance,
long resisted and never my own doctrine,
a body I would not be part of.
I all but say it: 'What have we done?
How shall we pay for this?'
But having a job to do I swallow
tears, guilt, these pallid secretions;
close the book; and carry it away
to answer someone's factual enquiry.

*7 p.m.*
In the desert the biggest tank battle
since World War II smashes on.
My friends are not sure whether their brothers
in Israel are still alive.
All day the skies roar with jets.
And I do not write political poems.

## House-talk

Through my pillow, through mattress, carpet, floor and ceiling,
sounds ooze up from the room below:
footsteps, chinking crockery, hot-water pipes groaning,
the muffled clunk of the refrigerator door,
and voices. They are trying to be quiet,
my son and his friends, home late in the evening.

Tones come softly filtered through the layers of padding.
I hear the words but not what the words are,
as on my radio when the batteries are fading.
Voices are reduced to a muted music:
Andrew's bass, his friend's tenor, the indistinguishable
light murmurs of the girls; occasional giggling.

Surely wood and plaster retain something
in their grain of all the essences they absorb?
This house has been lived in for ninety years,
nine by us. It has heard all manner of talking.
Its porous fabric must be saturated
with words. I offer it my peaceful breathing.

## Foreigner

These winds bully me:

I am to lie down in a ditch
quiet under the thrashing nettles
and pull the mud up to my chin.

Not that I would submit so
to one voice only;
but by the voices of these several winds
merged into a flowing fringe of tones
that swirl and comb over the hills
I am compelled.

I shall lie sound-proofed in the mud,
a huge caddis-fly larva,
a face floating upon Egyptian unguents
in a runnel at the bottom of England.

## In the Dingle Peninsula

We give ten pence to the old woman
and climb through nettles to the beehive hut.
You've been before. You're showing me prehistory,
ushering me into a stone cocoon.
I finger the corbelled wall and squat against it
bowing my back in submission to its curves.

The floor's washed rock: not even a scorchmark
as trace of the once-dwellers. But they're here,
closer than you, and trying to seduce me:
the arched stones burn against my shoulders,
my knees tingle, the cool air buzzes...
I drag my eyelids open and sleep-walk out.

'We're skeletons underneath' I've heard you say,
looking into coffins at neat arrangements
laid out in museums. We're skeletons.
I take the bones of your hand lightly in mine
through the dry flesh and walk unresisting,
willing to share it, over the peopled soil.


## In the Terai

Our throats full of dust, teeth harsh with it,
plastery sweat in our hair and nostrils,
we slam the flaps of the Landrover down
and think we choke on these roads.
Well, they will be better in time:
all along the dry riverbed
just as when we drove past this morning
men and women squatting under umbrellas
or cloth stretched over sticks, or nothing,
are splitting chipped stones to make smaller chips,
picking the fingernail-sized fragments
into graded heaps: roads by the handful.
We stop at the village and buy glasses of tea,
stewed and sweet; swallow dust with it
and are glad enough. The sun tilts lower.

Somewhere, surely, in this valley
under cool thatch mothers are feeding children
with steamy rice, leaning over them
to pour milk or water; the cups
tasting of earthenware, neutral, clean,
the young heads smelling only of hair.


# River

'... *I saw with infinite pleasure the great object of my mission; the long
sought for, majestic Niger, glittering to the morning sun, as broad as
the Thames at Westminster, and flowing slowly* to the eastward.'
MUNGO PARK
Travels in the Interior Districts of Africa

The strong image is always the river
was a line for the poem I never wrote
twenty years ago and never have written
of the green Wanganui under its willows
or the ice-blue milky-foaming Clutha
stopping my tremulous teenage heart.

But now when I cross Westminster Bridge
all that comes to mind is the Niger
a river Mungo Park invented for me
as he invented all those African villages
and a certain kind of astonishing silence –
the explorer having done the poet's job
and the poet feeling gratefully redundant.

*To and Fro*

## The Inner Harbour

*Paua-Shell*

Spilt petrol
oil on a puddle
the sea's colour-chart
porcelain, tie-dyed.
Tap the shell:
glazed calcium.

*Cat's-Eye*

Boss-eye, wall-eye, squinty lid
stony door for a sea-snail's tunnel

the long beach littered with them
domes of shell, discarded virginities

where the green girl wanders, willing
to lose hers to the right man

or to the wrong man, if he should raise
his frolic head above a sand dune

glossy-black-haired, and that smile on him

*Sea-Lives*

Under the sand at low tide
are whispers, hisses, long slithers,
bubbles, the suck of ingestion, a soft
snap: mysteries and exclusions.

Things grow on the dunes too –
pale straggle of lupin-bushes,
cutty-grass, evening primroses
puckering in the low light.

But the sea knows better.
Walk at the edge of its rich waves:
on the surface nothing shows;
underneath it is fat and fecund.


*Shrimping-Net*

Standing just under the boatshed
knee-deep in dappled water
sand-coloured legs and the sand itself
greenish in the lit ripples
watching the shrimps avoid her net
little flexible glass rockets
and the lifted mesh always empty
gauze and wire dripping sunlight

She is too tall to stand under
this house. It is a fantasy

And moving in from the bright outskirts
further under the shadowy floor
hearing a footstep creak above
her head brushing the rough timber
edging further bending her knees
creosote beams grazing her shoulder
the ground higher the roof lower
sand sifting on to her hair

She kneels in dark shallow water,
palms pressed upon shells and weed.


# Immigrant


November '63: eight months in London.
I pause on the low bridge to watch the pelicans:
they float swanlike, arching their white necks
over only slightly ruffled bundles of wings,
burying awkward beaks in the lake's water.

I clench cold fists in my Marks and Spencer's jacket
and secretly test my accent once again:
St James's Park; St James's Park; St James's Park.


111

## Settlers

First there is the hill        wooden houses
warm branches close against the face

Bamboo was in it somewhere
or another tall reed        and pines

Let it shift a little
settle into its own place

When we lived on the mountain
she said        But it was not
a mountain        nor they placed so high
nor where they came from a mountain
Manchester        and then the slow seas
hatches battened        a typhoon
so that all in the end became
mountains
            Steps to the venture
vehicles luggage bits of paper
all their people fallen away
shrunken into framed wedding groups
One knows at the time it can't be happening

Neighbours helped them build a house
what neighbours there were        and to farm
she and the boy much alone
her husband away in the town working
clipping hair        Her heart was weak
they said        ninety years with a weak heart
and such grotesque accidents
burns wrenches caustic soda
conspired against she had to believe

The waterfall        that was real
but she never mentioned the waterfall

After twelve years the slow reverse
from green wetness        cattle        weather
to somewhere at least        a township
air lower than the mountain's        calmer
a house with an orchard        peach and plum trees
tomato plants        their bruised scented leaves

and a third life        grandchildren
even the trip back to England at last

112

Then calmer still and closer in
suburbs       retraction into a city

We took her a cake for her birthday
going together       it was easier
Separately would have been kinder
and twice       For the same stories
rain cold now on the southerly harbour
wondering she must have been why
alone in the house or whether alone
her son in Europe       but someone
a man she thought in the locked room
where their things were stored       her things
about her       china the boxwood cabinet
photographs       Them's your Grandpa's people
and the noises in the room       a face

Hard to tell if she was frightened

Not simple       no       Much neglected
and much here omitted       Footnotes
Alice and her children gone ahead
the black sheep brother       the money
the whole slow long knotted tangle

And her fine straight profile too
her giggle       Eee       her dark eyes


## Going Back


There were always the places I couldn't spell, or couldn't find on maps –
too small, but swollen in family legend:
famous for bush-fires, near-drownings, or just the standard pioneer
grimness – twenty cows to milk by hand
before breakfast, and then a five-mile walk to school.
(Do I exaggerate? Perhaps; but hardly at all.)

They were my father's, mostly. One or two, until I was five,
rolled in and out of my own vision:
a wall with blackboards; a gate where I swung, the wind bleak in the telegraph
       wires;
Mother in this or that schoolhouse kitchen,
singing. And, in between, back to familiar bases:
Drury again, Christmas Days in grandparents' houses.

Suddenly no more New Zealand except in receding pictures
for years. And then we had it again, but different:
a city, big schools, my father a university teacher now.
But, being a nostalgic family, we went
in a newish car, along better roads, where once we'd rattled
in the Baby Austin over metal or clay surfaces, unsealed.

And we got most of it – nearly all the places that seemed to matter:
'Do you remember this path?' and 'There's the harbour
we had to cross in the launch when you were a new baby
and a storm came up, and we thought we'd go under.'
Here and there a known vista or the familiar angle
of a room to a garden made my own memories tingle.

But nostalgia-time ran out as I grew older and more busy
and became a parent myself, and left the country
for longer than they had left it; with certain things undone:
among them, two holes in the map empty.
Now I've stitched them in. I have the fabric complete,
the whole of the North Island pinned out flat.

First my own most haunting obsession, the school at Tokorangi.
It was I who spotted the turning off the road,
identified the trees, the mound, the contours programmed into my system
when I was five, and the L-shaped shed
echoing for two of us with voices; for the rest
an object of polite historical interest.

And a week later, one for my father, smaller and more remote,
a square wooden box on a little hill.
The door creaked rustily open. He stood in the entrance porch, he touched
the tap he'd so often turned, the very nail
where sixty years ago the barometer had hung
to be read at the start of each patterned morning.

Two bits of the back-blocks, then, two differently rural settings
for schools, were they? Schools no longer.
Left idle by the motorised successors of the pioneers
each had the same still mask to offer:
broken windows, grassy silence, all the children gone away,
and classrooms turned into barns for storing hay.

# Instead of an Interview

The hills, I told them; and water, and the clear air
(not yielding to more journalistic probings);
and a river or two, I could say, and certain bays
and ah, those various and incredible hills...

And all my family still in the one city
within walking distances of each other
through streets I could follow blind. My school was gone
and half my Thorndon smashed for the motorway
but every corner revealed familiar settings
for the dreams I'd not bothered to remember –
ingrained; ingrown; incestuous: like the country.

And another city offering me a lover
and quite enough friends to be going on with;
bookshops; galleries; gardens; fish in the sea;
lemons and passionfruit growing free as the bush.
Then the bush itself; and the wild grand south;
and wooden houses in occasional special towns.

And not a town or a city I could live in.
Home, as I explained to a weeping niece,
home is London; and England, Ireland, Europe.
I have come home with a suitcase full of stones –
of shells and pebbles, pottery, pieces of bark:
here they lie around the floor of my study
as I telephone a cable 'Safely home'

and moments later, thinking of my dears,
wish the over-resonant word cancelled:
'Arrived safely' would have been clear enough,
neutral, kinder. But another loaded word
creeps up now to interrogate me.
By going back to look, after thirteen years,
have I made myself for the first time an exile?

# Londoner

Scarcely two hours back in the country
and I'm shopping in East Finchley High Road
in a cotton skirt, a cardigan, jandals –
or flipflops as people call them here,
where February's winter. Aren't I cold?
The neighbours in their overcoats are smiling
at my smiles and not at my bare toes:
they know me here.
                  I hardly know myself,
yet. It takes me until Monday evening,
walking from the office after dark
to Westminster Bridge. It's cold, it's foggy,
the traffic's as abominable as ever,
and there across the Thames is County Hall,
that uninspired stone body, floodlit.
It makes me laugh. In fact, it makes me sing.


# To Marilyn from London

You did London early, at nineteen:
the basement room, the geriatric nursing,
cinema queues, modish fall-apart dresses,
and marriage at Stoke Newington Registry Office,
Spring 1955, on the rebound.

Marrying was what we did in those days.
And soon enough you were back in Wellington
with your eye-shadow and your Edith Piaf records
buying kitchen furniture on hire-purchase
and writing novels when the babies were asleep.

Somehow you're still there, I'm here; and now
Sarah arrives: baby-faced like you then,
second of your four blonde Christmas-tree fairies,
nineteen; competent; with her one suitcase
and her two passports. It begins again.

# BELOW LOUGHRIGG

(1979)

# Below Loughrigg

The power speaks only out of sleep and blackness
no use looking for the sun
what is not present cannot be illumined

Katherine's lungs, remember, eaten by disease
but Mary's fingers too
devoured and she goes on writing

The water speaks from the rocks, the cavern speaks,
where water halloos through it
this happens also in darkness

A steep bit here, up from the valley
to the terraces, the path eroded by water
Now listen for the voice

These things wane with the vital forces
he said, little having waned in him
except faith, and anger had replaced it

One force can be as good as another
we may not think so; but channelled
in ways it has eaten out; issuing

into neither a pool nor the sea
but a shapely lake afloat with wooded islands
a real water and multiplied on maps

which can be read in the sunlight; for the sun
will not be stopped from visiting
and the lake exists and the wind sings over it.

# Three Rainbows in One Morning

It is not only the eye that is astonished.

Predictable enough in rainbow weather,
the drenched air saturated with colours,
that over each valley should hang an arc
and over this long lake the longest.

Knowing how it happens is no defence.
They stop the car and are delighted.

But some centre of gravity is upset,
some internal gauge or indicator
fed once again with the routine question
'This place, now: would it be possible
to live here?' buzzes, rolls
and registers 'Yes. Yes; perhaps.'


# Binoculars

'What are you looking at?' 'Looking.'
High screed sides; possibly a raven,
he thought. Bracken a fuzz of rust
on the iron slopes of the fell
(off the edge of their map, nameless)
and the sky clean after rain.
At last he put the binoculars down,
drove on further to the north.

It was a good day in the end:
the cold lake lapping against pines,
and the square-built northern town idle
in sunlight. It seemed they had crossed borders.
Driving south became a return
to nests of trees in ornamental colours.
Leaving, he left her the binoculars
to watch her wrens and robins until spring.

# Paths

I am the dotted lines on the map:
footpaths exist only when they are walked on.
I am gravel tracks through woodland; I am
field paths, the muddy ledge by the stream,
the stepping-stones. I am the grassy lane
open between waist-high bracken where sheep
fidget. I am the track to the top
skirting and scaling rocks. I am the cairn.

Here on the brow of the world I stop,
set my stone face to the wind, and turn
to each wide quarter. I am that I am.


# Mid-point

Finding I've walked halfway around Loughrigg
I wonder: do I still want to go on?
Normally, yes. But now, hardly recovered
from 'flu, and feeling slightly faint in the sun,
dazzled by early spring, I hesitate.
How far is it around this sprawling fell?
I've come perhaps three miles. Will it be four,
or less, the Grasmere way? It's hard to tell.
The ups and downs undo one's feel for distance;
the soaring views distract from what's at hand.
But here's the tarn, spangled with quick refractions
of sunlight, to remind me where I stand.
There's no way on or back except by walking
and whichever route I choose involves a climb.
On, then, no question: if I find myself
lacking in energy, at least I've time.
It will be cooler when I'm facing north –
frost often lingers there – and I'll take heart
from gazing down again on Rydal Water.
The point of no return was at the start.

## The Spirit of the Place

Mist like evaporating stone
smudges the bracken. Not much further now.
Below on the other side of the village
Windermere tilts its pewter face
over towards me as I move downhill.
I've walked my boots clean in gravelly streams;
picking twigs of glittering holly
to take home I've lacerated my fingers
(it serves me right: holly belongs on trees).
Now as the early dusk descends behind me
dogs in the kennels above Nook Lane
are barking, growling, hysterical at something;
and from the housing estate below
a deep mad voice bellows 'Wordsworth! Wordsworth!'


## The Vale of Grasmere

These coloured slopes ought to inspire,
as much as anything, discretion:
think of the egotisms laid bare,
the shy campaigns of self-projection
tricked out as visits to Dove Cottage
tellingly rendered. Every year
some poet comes on pilgrimage
along these valleys. Read his verses:
each bud of delicate perception
sprouts from a blossoming neurosis
too well watered by Grasmere –
in which he sees his own reflection.
He sits beside a tarn or ghyll
sensitively eating chocolate
and eyes Helm Crag or Rydal Fell
plotting some novel way to use it.
Most of the rocks are wreathed by now
with faded rags of fluttering soul.
But the body finds another function
for crags and fells, as Wordsworth knew
himself: they offer hands and feet
their own creative work to do.
'I climb because I can't write,'
one honest man said. Better so.

# Letter to Alistair Campbell

Those thorn trees in your poems, Alistair,
we have them here. Also the white cauldron,
the basin of your waterfall. I stare
at Stock Ghyll Force and can't escape your words.
You'd love this place: it's your Central Otago
in English dress – the bony land's the same;
and if the Cromwell Gorge is doomed to go
under a lake, submerging its brave orchards
for cheap electric power, this is where
you'd find a subtly altered image of it,
its cousin in another hemisphere:
the rivers gentler, hills more widely splayed
but craggy enough. Well. Some year you'll manage
to travel north, as I two years ago
went south. Meanwhile our sons are of an age
to do it for us: Andrew's been with you
in Wellington. Now I'm about to welcome
our firstborn Gregory to England. Soon,
if Andrew will surrender him, he'll come
from grimy fetid London – still my base,
I grant you, still my centre, but with air
that chokes me now each time I enter it –
to this pure valley where no haze but weather
obscures the peaks from time to time, clean rain
or tender mist (forgive my lyrical
effusiveness: Wordsworthian locutions
are carried on the winds in what I call
my this year's home. You've had such fits yourself.)
So: Gregory will come to Ambleside
and see the lakes, the Rothay, all these waters.
Two years ago he sat with me beside
the Clutha, on those rocks where you and I
did our first timid courting. Symmetry
pleases me; correspondences and chimes
are not just ornament. And if I try
too hard to emphasise the visual echoes
between a place of mine and one of yours
it's not only for art's sake but for friendship:
five years of marriage, twenty of divorce
are our foundation. It occurred to me
in August, round about the twenty-third,
that we'd deprived ourselves of cake, champagne,
a silver tea-service, the family gathered –

I almost felt I ought to send a card.
Well, that can wait: it won't be long before
you have my blessings on your twentieth year
with Meg; but let this, in the meantime, be for
our older link through places and your poems.


## Declensions


Snow on the tops: half the day I've sat at the window
   staring at fells made suddenly remote
by whiteness that disguises them as high mountains
   reared behind the bracken-covered slopes
of others whose colour yesterday was theirs.
   In the middle distance, half-stripped trees
have shed pink stains on the grass beneath them.
   That other pinkness over Windermere
is the setting sun through cloud. And in the foreground
   birds act out their various natures
around the food I've set on the terrace wall:
   the plump chaffinch eats on steadily
even in a hail-shower; tits return when it's over
   to swing on their bacon-rind; a dunnock hops
picking stray seeds; and the territorial robin,
   brisk, beady-eyed, sees them all off.
I am not at all sure that this is the real world
   but I am looking at it very closely.
Is landscape serious? Are birds? But they are fading
   in dusk, in the crawling darkness. Enough.
Knowing no way to record what is famous
   precisely for being unrecordable,
I draw the curtains and settle to my book:
   Dr William Smith's *First Greek Course,*
Exercise Fourteen: third declension nouns.
   My letters, awkward from years of non-use,
sprinkle over the page like birds' footprints,
   quaint thorny symbols, pecked with accents:
as I turn the antique model sentences:
   The vines are praised by the husbandmen.
The citizens delight in strife and faction.
   The harbour has a difficult entrance.

# Weathering

Literally thin-skinned, I suppose, my face
catches the wind off the snow-line and flushes
with a flush that will never wholly settle. Well:
that was a metropolitan vanity,
wanting to look young for ever, to pass.

I was never a Pre-Raphaelite beauty,
nor anything but pretty enough to satisfy
men who need to be seen with passable women.
But now that I am in love with a place
which doesn't care how I look, or if I'm happy,

happy is how I look, and that's all.
My hair will turn grey in any case,
my nails chip and flake, my waist thicken,
and the years work all their usual changes.
If my face is to be weather-beaten as well

that's little enough lost, a fair bargain
for a year among lakes and fells, when simply
to look out of my window at the high pass
makes me indifferent to mirrors and to what
my soul may wear over its new complexion.

# Going out from Ambleside

### 1

He is lying on his back watching a kestrel,
his head on the turf, hands under his neck,
warm air washing over his face,
and the sky clear blue where the kestrel hovers.

A person comes with a thermometer.
He watches a ceiling for three minutes.
The person leaves. He watches the kestrel again
his head pressed back among the harebells.

**2**

Today he will go over to Langdale.
He springs lightly in his seven-league boots
around the side of Loughrigg
bouncing from rock to rock in the water-courses
evading slithery clumps of weed, skipping
like a sheep among the rushes
coursing along the curved path upward
through bracken, over turf to a knoll
and across it, around and on again
higher and higher, glowing with exaltation
up to where it all opens out.
That was easy. And it was just the beginning.


**3**

They bring him tea or soup.
He does not notice it. He is busy
identifying fungi in Skelghyll Wood,
comparing them with the pictures in his mind:
Purple Blewit, Yellow Prickle Fungus,
Puffball, Russula, two kinds of Boletus –
the right weather for them.
And what are these little pearly knobs
pressing up among the leaf-mould?
He treads carefully over damp grass,
patches of brilliant moss, pine-needles,
hoping for a Fly Agaric.
Scarlet catches his eye. But it was only
reddening leaves on a bramble.
And here's bracken, fully brown,
and acorns. It must be October.


**4**

What is this high wind coming,
leaves leaping from the trees to bite his face?
A storm. He should have noticed the signs.
But it doesn't matter. Ah, turn into it,
let the rain bite on the warm skin too.


**5**

Cold. Suddenly cold. Or hot.
A pain under his breastbone;
and his feet are bare. This is curious.

Someone comes with an injection.

6

They have brought Kurt Schwitters to see him,
a clumsy-looking man in a beret
asking for bits of stuff to make a collage.
Here, take my stamp-collection
and the letters my children wrote from school
and this photograph of my wife. She's dead now.
You are dead too, Kurt Schwitters.


7

This is a day for sailing, perhaps,
coming down from the fells to lake-level;
or for something gentler: for idling
with a fishing-line and listening to water;
or just for lying in a boat
on a summer evening in the lee of a shore
letting the wind steer, leaving the hull
to its own course, the waves to lap it along.


8

But where now suddenly? Dawn light,
peaks around him, shadowy and familiar,
tufts of mist over a tarn below.
Somehow he is higher than he intended;
and careless, giddy, running to the edge
and over it, straight down on splintery scree
leaning back on his boots, a ski-run
scattering chips of slate, a skid with no stopping
down through the brief mist and into the tarn.


9

Tomorrow perhaps he will think about Helvellyn...

# SELECTED POEMS

(1983)

## In the Unicorn, Ambleside

I want to have ice-skates and a hoop
and to have lived all my life in the same house
above Stock; and to skate on Lily Tarn
every winter, because it always freezes –
or always did freeze when you were a girl.

I want to believe your tales about Wordsworth –
'Listen to what the locals say,' you tell me:
'He drank in every pub from here to Ullswater,
and had half the girls. We all know that.'
I want not to know better, out of books.

I sit in the pub with my posh friends, talking
literature and publishing as usual.
Some of them really do admire Wordsworth.
But they won't listen to you. I listen:
how can I get you to listen to me?

I can't help not being local;
but I'm here, aren't I? And this afternoon
Jane and I sat beside Lily Tarn
watching the bright wind attack the ice.
None of you were up there skating.


## Downstream

Last I became a raft of green bubbles
meshed into the miniature leaves
of that small pondweed (has it a name?)
that lies green-black on the stream's face:
a sprinkle of round seeds, if you mistake it,
or of seed-hulls holding air among them.

I was those globules; there they floated –
all there was to do was to float
on the degenerate stream, suburbanised,
the mill-stream where it is lost among houses
and hardly moving, swilling just a little
to and fro if the wind blows it.

But it did move, and I moved on, drifting
until I entered the river
where I was comported upon a tear's fashion
blending into the long water
until you would not see that there had been
tear or bubble or any round thing ever.


## The Hillside

Tawny-white as a ripe hayfield.
But it is heavy with frost, not seed.

It frames him for you as he sits by the window,
his hair white also, a switch of silver.

He pours you another glass of wine,
laughs at your shy anecdotes, quietly caps them,

is witty as always; glows as hardly ever,
his back to the rectangles of glass.

The snow holds off. Clouds neither pass nor lower
their flakes on to the hill's pale surface.

Tell him there is green beneath it still:
he will almost, for this afternoon, believe you.


## This Ungentle Music

Angry Mozart: the only kind for now.
Tinkling would appal on such an evening,
summer, when the possible things to do
are: rip all weeds out of the garden,
butcher the soft redundancy of the hedge
in public; and go, when the light slackens,
to stamp sharp echoes along the street

mouthing futilities: 'A world where...'
as if there were a choice of other worlds
than this one in which it is the case
that nothing can stamp out leukaemia.

So Malcolm has had to die at twenty,
humming off on a low blue flame
of heroin, a terminal kindness.

Wild rock howls on someone's record.
Fog sifts over the young moon.


## The Ring

Then in the end she didn't marry him
and go to Guyana; the politics of the thing
had to be considered, and her daughter,
too English by now. But she found the ring,

her mourned and glittering hoop of diamonds,
not lost in a drain after all
but wrenched and twisted into a painful oblong
jammed between the divan-bed and the wall.


## Corrosion

It was going to be a novel
about his friend, the seventeen-year-old
with the pale hair ('younger brother';
that day on the river-bank).
                              Until
he thought perhaps a sonnet-sequence:
more stripped-down, more crystalline.

Or just one sonnet even, one
imaging of the slight bones
almost visible through that skin,
a fine articulation of golden wire.

The bones were what he most held to,
talking about them often: of how
if David (we could call him)
were to have been drenched with acid
and his skin burnt off, the luminous flesh
burnt, it would make no difference.

The slow acid of age
with its lesser burning
he may also have touched on.


## 4 May 1979

Doom and sunshine stream over the garden.
The mindless daffodils are nodding
bright primped heads at the Tory sky:
such blue elation of spring air!
Such freshness! – the oxides and pollutants
hardly yet more than a sweet dust.
Honesty, that mistaken plant,
has opened several dozen purple buds,
about which the bees are confident.
It might be 1970; it might be 1914.


## Madmen

Odd how the seemingly maddest of men –
sheer loonies, the classically paranoid,
violently possessive about their secrets,
whispered after from corners, terrified
of poison in their coffee, driven frantic
(whether for or against him) by discussion of God,
peculiar, to say the least, about their mothers –
return to their gentle senses in bed.

Suddenly straightforward, they perform
with routine confidence, neither afraid
that their partner will turn and bite their balls off
nor groping under the pillow for a razor-blade;
eccentric only in their conversation,
which rambles on about the meaning of a word
they used in an argument in 1969,
they leave their women grateful, relieved, and bored.

## Shakespeare's Hotspur

He gurgled beautifully on television,
playing your death, that Shakespearian actor.
Blood glugged under his tongue, he gagged on
words, as you did. Hotspur, Hotspur:
it was an arrow killed you, not a prince,
not Hal clashing over you in his armour,
stabbing featly for the cameras, and your face
unmaimed. You fell into the hands of Shakespeare,
were given a lovely fluency,
undone, redone, made his creature.
In life you never found it easy
to volley phrases off into the future.
And as for your death-scene, that hot day
at Shrewsbury you lifted your visor:
a random arrow smashed into your eye
and mummed your tongue-tied mouth for ever.

## Nature Table

The tadpoles won't keep still in the aquarium;
Ben's tried seven times to count them –
thirty-two, thirty-three, wriggle, wriggle –
all right, he's got better things to do.

Heidi stares into the tank, wearing
a snail on her knuckle like a ring.
She can see purple clouds in the water,
a sky for the tadpoles in their world.

Matthew's drawing a worm. Yesterday
he put one down Elizabeth's neck.
But these are safely locked in the wormery
eating their mud; he's tried that too.

Laura sways with her nose in a daffodil,
drunk on pollen, her eyes tight shut.
The whole inside of her head is filling
with a slow hum of fizzy yellow.

Tom squashes his nose against the window.
He hopes it may look like a snail's belly
to the thrush outside. But is not attacked:
the thrush is happy on the bird-table.

The wind ruffles a chaffinch's crest
and gives the sparrows frilly grey knickers
as they squabble over their seeds and bread.
The sun swings in and out of clouds.

Ben's constructing a wigwam of leaves
for the snails. Heidi whispers to the tadpoles
'Promise you won't start eating each other!'
Matthew's rather hoping they will.

A wash of sun sluices the window,
bleaches Tom's hair blonder, separates
Laura from her daffodil with a sneeze,
and sends the tadpoles briefly frantic;

until the clouds flop down again
grey as wet canvas. The wind quickens,
birds go flying, window-glass rattles,
pellets of hail are among the birdseed.


## Revision


It has to be learned afresh
every new start or every season,
revised like the languages that faltered
after I left school or when I stopped
going every year to Italy. Or
like how to float on my back, swimming,
not swimming, ears full of sea-water;
like the taste of the wine at first communion
(because each communion is the first);
like dancing and how to ride a horse –
can I still? Do I still want to?

The sun is on the leaves again;
birds are making rather special noises;
and I can see for miles and miles
even with my eyes closed.

So yes: teach it to me again.

# Influenza

Dreamy with illness
we are Siamese twins
fused at the groin
too languid to stir.

We sprawl transfixed
remote from the day.
The window is open.
The curtain flutters.

Epics of sound-effects
ripple timelessly:
a dog is barking
in vague slow bursts;

cars drone; someone
is felling a tree.
Forests could topple
between the axe-blows.

Draughts idle over
our burning faces
and my fingers over
the drum in your ribs.

You lick my eyelid:
the fever grips us.
We shake in its hands
until it lets go.

Then you gulp cold water
and make of your mouth
a wet cool tunnel.
I slake my lips at it.

# Crab

Late at night we wrench open a crab;
flesh bursts out of its cup

in pastel colours. The dark fronds attract me:
Poison, you say, Dead Men's Fingers –

don't put them in your mouth, stop!
They brush over my tongue, limp and mossy,

until you snatch them from me, as you snatch
yourself, gently, if I come too close.

Here are the permitted parts of the crab,
wholesome on their nests of lettuce

and we are safe again in words.
All day the kitchen will smell of sea.


# Eclipse

Today the Dog of Heaven swallowed the sun.
Birds twanged for the dusk and fell silent,
one puzzled flock after another –
African egrets; parakeets; Chinese crows.

But firecrackers fended the beast off:
he spat it out, his hot glorious gobful.
Now it will be ours again tomorrow
for the birds here to rediscover at dawn.

What they chirrup to it will ring like praise
from blackbirds, thrushes, eleven kinds of finches,
that certain tribesmen in the south of China
have not unlearnt their pre-republican ways.

## On the Border

Dear posterity, it's 2 a.m.
and I can't sleep for the smothering heat,
or under mosquito nets. The others
are swathed in theirs, humid and sweating,
long white packets on rows of chairs
(no bunks. The building isn't finished).

I prowled in the dark back room for water
and came outside for a cigarette
and a pee in waist-high leafy scrub.
The moon is brilliant: the same moon,
I have to believe, as mine in England
or theirs in the places where I'm not.

Knobbly trees mark the horizon,
black and angular, with no leaves:
blossoming flame trees; and behind them
soft throbbings come from the village.
Birds or animals croak and howl;
the river rustles; there could be snakes.

I don't care. I am standing here,
posterity, on the face of the earth,
letting the breeze blow up my nightdress,
writing in English, as I do,
in all this tropical non-silence.
Now let me tell you about the elephants.

## The Prize-winning Poem

It will be typed, of course, and not all in capitals: it will use upper and lower case
in the normal way; and where a space is usual it will have a space.
It will probably be on white paper, or possibly blue, but almost certainly not pink.
It will not be decorated with ornamental scroll-work in coloured ink,
nor will a photograph of the poet be glued above his or her name,
and still less a snap of the poet's children frolicking in a jolly game.
The poem will not be about feeling lonely and being fifteen
and unless the occasion of the competition is a royal jubilee it will not be
       about the queen.

It will not be the first poem the author has written in his life
and will probably not be about the death of his daughter, son or wife
because although to write such elegies fulfils a therapeutic need
in large numbers they are deeply depressing for the judges to read.
The title will not be 'Thoughts' or 'Life' or 'I Wonder Why'
or 'The Bunny-Rabbit's Birthday Party' or 'In Days of Long Gone By'.
'Tis and 'twas, o'er and e'er, and such poetical contractions will not be found
in the chosen poem. Similarly clichés will not abound:
dawn will not herald another bright new day, nor dew sparkle like diamonds
      in a dell,
nor trees their arms upstretch. Also the poet will be able to spell.
Large meaningless concepts will not be viewed with favour: myriad is out;
infinity is becoming suspect; aeons and galaxies are in some doubt.
Archaisms and inversions will not occur; nymphs will not their fate bemoan.
Apart from this there will be no restrictions upon the style or tone.
What is required is simply the masterpiece we'd all write if we could.
There is only one prescription for it: it's got to be good.

## An Emblem

Someone has nailed a lucky horse-shoe
beside my door while I was out –
or is it a loop of rubber? No:
it's in two sections. They glide about,
silently undulating: two
slugs in a circle, tail to snout.

The ends link up: it's a shiny quoit
of rippling slug-flesh, thick as a snake,
liquorice-black against the white
paint; a pair of wetly-nak-
ed tubes. It doesn't seem quite right
to watch what kind of love they'll make.

But who could resist? I'll compromise
and give them a little time alone
to nuzzle each other, slide and ooze
into conjunction on their own;
surely they're experts, with such bodies,
each a complete erogenous zone –

self-lubricating, swelling smooth
and boneless under grainy skin.
Ten minutes, then, for them to writhe
in privacy, to slither in-
to position, to arrange each lithe
tapered hose-pipe around its twin.

All right, now, slugs, I'm back; time's up.
And what a pretty coupling I find!
They're swinging from the wall by a rope
of glue, spun out of their combined
mucus and anchored at the top.
It lets them dangle, intertwined,

formally perfect, like some emblem:
heraldic serpents coiled in a twist.
But just in case their pose may seem
immodest or exhibitionist
they've dressed themselves in a cloud of foam,
a frothy veil for love-in-a-mist.


## Piano Concerto in E Flat Major


In her 1930s bob or even, perhaps,
if she saw something quainter as her fashion,
long thick hair in a plait, the music student
showed her composition to her tutor;
and she aroused, or this enhanced, his passion.

He quoted from it in his new concerto,
offering back to her as homage
those several bars of hers the pianist plays
in the second movement: part of what she dreamed
re-translated, marked more with his image.

But the seven steady notes of the main theme
are his alone. Did the romance go well?
Whether he married her's recorded somewhere
in books. The wistful strings, the determined
percussion, the English cadences, don't tell.

# Villa Isola Bella

*'You will find Isola Bella in pokerwork on my heart'*
KATHERINE MANSFIELD to JOHN MIDDLETON MURRY
10 November 1920 (inscribed outside the
Katherine Mansfield memorial room in Menton)

Your villa, Katherine, but not your room,
and not much of your garden. Goods trains boom
all night, a dozen metres from the bed
where tinier tremors hurtle through my head.
The ghost of your hot flat-iron burns my lung;
my throat's all scorching lumps. I grope among
black laurels and the shadowy date-palm, made
like fans of steel, each rustling frond a blade,
across the gravel to the outside loo
whose light won't wake my sleeping sister. You
smoked shameless Turkish all through your TB.
I drag at Silk Cut filters, duty-free,
then gargle sensibly with Oraldene
and spit pink froth. Not blood: it doesn't mean,
like your spat scarlet, that I'll soon be dead –
merely that pharmacists are fond of red.
I'm hardly sick at all. There's just this fuzz
that blurs and syncopates the singing buzz
of crickets, frogs, and traffic in my ears:
a nameless fever, atavistic fears.
Disease is portable: my bare half-week
down here's hatched no maladie exotique;
I brought my tinglings with me, just as you
brought ragged lungs and work you burned to do;
and, as its fuel, your ecstasy-prone heart.
Whatever haunts my bloodstream didn't start
below your villa, in our genteel den
(till lately a pissoir for passing men).
But your harsh breathing and impatient face,
bright with consumption, must have left a trace
held in the air. Well, Katherine, Goodnight:
let's try to sleep. I'm switching out the light.
Watch me through tepid darkness, wavering back
past leaves and stucco and their reverent plaque
to open what was not in fact your door
and find my narrow mattress on the floor.

# Lantern Slides

### 1

'You'll have to put the little girl down.'
Is it a little girl who's bundled
in both our coats against my shoulder,
buried among the trailing cloth?

It's a big haul up to the quay,
my other arm heavy with luggage,
the ship lurching. Who's my burden?
She had a man's voice this morning.

### 2

Floods everywhere. Monsoon rain
syphoning down into the valley.
When it stops you see the fungus
hugely coiling out of the grass.

Really, in such a derelict lane
you wouldn't expect so many cars,
black and square, driving jerkily.
It's not as if we were near a village.

### 3

Now here's the bridal procession:
the groom pale and slender in black
and his hair black under his hat-brim;
is that a frock-coat he's wearing?

The bride's as tall as his trouser pocket;
she hoists her arm to hold his hand,
and rucks her veil askew. Don't,
for your peace of mind, look under it.

### 4

The ceremony will be in a cavern,
a deep deserted underground station
built like a theatre; and so it is:
ochre-painted, proscenium-arched.

The men have ribbons on their hatbands;
there they are, behind the grille,
receding with her, minute by minute,
shrivelling down the empty track.

# Dreaming

'Oblivion, that's all. I never dream,' he said –
proud of it, another immunity,
another removal from the standard frame which she
inhabited, dreaming beside him of a dead
woman tucked neatly into a small bed,
a cot or a child's bunk, unexpectedly
victim of some friend or lover. 'Comfort me,'
said the dreamer, 'I need to be comforted.'
He did that, not bothering to comprehend,
and she returned to her story: a doctor came
to identify the placid corpse in her dream.
It was obscure; but glancing towards the end
she guessed that killer and lover and doctor were the same;
proving that things are ultimately what they seem.

# Street Song

Pink Lane, Strawberry Lane, Pudding Chare:
someone is waiting, I don't know where;
hiding among the nursery names,
he wants to play peculiar games.

In Leazes Terrace or Leazes Park
someone is loitering in the dark,
feeling the giggles rise in his throat
and fingering something under his coat.

He could be sidling along Forth Lane
to stop some girl from catching her train,
or stalking the grounds of the RVI
to see if a student nurse goes by.

In Belle Grove Terrace or Fountain Row
or Hunter's Road he's raring to go –
unless he's the quiet shape you'll meet
on the cobbles in Back Stowell Street.

Monk Street, Friars Street, Gallowgate
are better avoided when it's late.
Even in Sandhill and the Side
there are shadows where a man could hide.

So don't go lightly along Darn Crook
because the Ripper's been brought to book.
Wear flat shoes, and be ready to run:
remember, sisters, there's more than one.


## Across the Moor


He had followed her across the moor,
taking shortcuts, light and silent
on the grass where the fair had been –
and in such weather, the clouds dazzling
in a loud warm wind, who'd hear?

He was almost up with her
at the far side, near the road,
when a man with a blotched skin
brought his ugly dogs towards them.
It could have been an interruption.
And as she closed the cattle-gate
in his face almost, he saw
that she was not the one, and let her go.

There had been something. It was
not quite clear yet, he thought.
So he loitered on the bridge,
idle now, the wind in his hair,
gazing over into the stream
of traffic; and for a moment
it seemed to him he saw it there.

# Bethan and Bethany

Bethan and Bethany sleep in real linen –
avert your covetous eyes, you starers;
their counterpanes are of handmade lace:
this is a civilised country.

If it is all just one big suburb
gliding behind its freezing mist
it is a decorated one;
it is of brick, and it is tidy.

Above the court-house portico
Justice holds her scales in balance;
the seventeenth-century church is locked
but the plaque outside has been regilded.

Bethan and Bethany, twelve and eleven,
bared their eyes to the television
rose-red-neon-lit, and whispered
in their related languages.

Guess now, through the frilled net curtains,
which belongs here and which doesn't.
Each of them owns the same records;
this is an international culture.

The yobs in the street hoot like all yobs,
hawk and whistle and use no language.
Bethan and Bethany stir in their sleep.
The brindled cat walks on their stomachs.

# Blue Glass

The underworld of children becomes the overworld
when Janey or Sharon shuts the attic door
on a sunny afternoon and tiptoes in sandals
that softly waffle-print the dusty floor

to the cluttered bed below the skylight,
managing not to sneeze as she lifts
newspapers, boxes, gap-stringed tennis-racquets
and a hamster's cage to the floor, and shifts

the tasselled cover to make a clean surface
and a pillow to be tidy under her head
before she straightens, mouths the dark sentence,
and lays herself out like a mummy on the bed.

Her wrists are crossed. The pads of her fingertips
trace the cold glass emblem where it lies
like a chain of hailstones melting in the dips
above her collarbones. She needs no eyes

to see it: the blue bead necklace, of sapphire
or lapis, or of other words she knows
which might mean blueness: amethyst, azure,
chalcedony can hardly say how it glows.

She stole it. She tells herself that she found it.
It's hers now. It owns her. She slithers among
its globular teeth, skidding on blue pellets.
Ice-beads flare and blossom on her tongue,

turn into flowers, populate the spaces
around and below her. The attic has become
her bluebell wood. Among their sappy grasses
the light-fringed gas-flames of bluebells hum.

They lift her body like a cloud of petals.
High now, floating, this is what she sees:
granular bark six inches from her eyeballs;
the wood of rafters is the wood of trees.

Her breathing moistens the branches' undersides;
the sunlight in an interrupted shaft
warms her legs and lulls her as she rides
on air, a slender and impossible raft

of bones and flesh; and whether it is knowledge
or a limpid innocence on which she feeds
for power hasn't mattered. She turns the necklace
kindly in her fingers, and soothes the beads.

# Mary Magdalene and the Birds

### 1

Tricks and tumbles are my trade; I'm
all birds to all men.
I switch voices, adapt my features,
do whatever turn you fancy.
All that is constant is my hair:

plumage, darlings, beware of it.

### 2

Blackbird: that's the one to watch —
or he is, with his gloss and weapon.
Not a profession for a female,
his brown shadow. Thrush is better,
cunning rehearser among the leaves,
and speckle-breasted, maculate.

### 3

A wound of some kind. All that talk
of the pelican, self-wounding,
feeding his brood from an ever-bleeding
bosom turns me slightly sick.

But seriousness can light upon
the flightiest. This tingling ache,
nicer than pain, is a blade-stroke:
not my own, but I let it happen.

### 4

What is balsam? What is nard?
Sweetnesses from the sweet life,
obsolete, fit only for wasting.

I groom you with this essence. Wash it
down the drain with tears and water.
We are too human. Let it pass.

## 5

*With my body I thee worship*:
breast on stone lies the rockdove
cold on that bare nest, cooing
its low call, unlulled,
restless for the calling to cease.


## 6

Mary Magdalene sang in the garden.
It was a swansong, said the women,
for his downdrift on the river.

It sounded more of the spring curlew
or a dawn sky full of larks,
watery trillings you could drown in.

# HOTSPUR

(1986)

*a ballad for music by*
GILLIAN WHITEHEAD

# I

There is no safety
there is no shelter
the dark dream
will drag us under.

\*

I married a man of metal and fire,
quick as a cat, and wild:
Harry Percy the Hotspur,
the Earl of Northumberland's child.

He rode to battle at fourteen years.
He won his prickly name.
His talking is a halting spate,
his temper a trembling flame.

He has three castles to his use,
north of the Roman Wall:
Alnwick, Berwick, Warkworth –
and bowers for me in them all.

I may dance and carol and sing;
I may go sweetly dressed
in silks that suit the lady I am;
I may lie on his breast;

and peace may perch like a hawk on my wrist
but can never come tame to hand,
wed as I am to a warrior
in a wild warring land.

\*

High is his prowess
in works of chivalry,
noble his largesse,
franchyse and courtesy.

All this wilderness
owes him loyalty;
and deathly rashness
bears him company.

## II

The Earl of Douglas clattered south
with Scottish lords and men at arms.
He smudged our tall Northumberland skies
black with the smoke of burning farms.

My Hotspur hurried to halt his course;
Newcastle was their meeting-place.
Douglas camped on the Castle Leazes;
they met in combat, face to face.

It was as fair as any fight,
but Douglas drew the lucky chance:
he hurled my husband from his saddle,
stunned on the earth, and snatched his lance.

I weep to think what Harry saw
as soon as he had strength to stand:
the silken pennon of the Percies
flaunted in a foreign hand.

'Sir, I shall bear this token off
and set it high on my castle gate.'
'Sir, you shall not pass the bounds
of the county till you meet your fate.'

The city held against the siege;
the Scots were tired and forced to turn.
They tramped away with all their gear
to wait my lord at Otterburn.


## III

I sit with my ladies in the turret-room
late in the day, and watch them sewing.
Their fingers flicker over the linen;
mine lie idle with remembering.

Last night the moon travelled through cloud
growing and shrinking minute by minute,
one day from fullness, a pewter cup
of white milk with white froth on it.

These August days are long to pass.
I have watched the berries on the rowan
creeping from green towards vermilion,
slow as my own body to ripen.

I was eight years old when we married,
a child-bride for a boy warrior.
Eight more years dragged past before
they thought me fit for the bridal chamber.

Now I am a woman, and proved to be so:
I carry the tender crop of our future;
while he pursues what he cannot leave,
drawn to danger by his lion's nature.

Daylight fades in the turret-slit;
my ladies lay aside their needles.
They murmur and yawn and fold away
the fine-worked linen to dress a cradle.

And I should rest before the harvest moon
rises to dazzle me. But now
I stitch and cannot think of sleep.
What should I be sewing for tomorrow?


IV

It fell about the Lammastide –
the people put it in a song –
the famous fray at Otterburn,
fought by moonlight, hard and long.

The Percies wore the silver crescent;
the moon was a full moon overhead.
Harry and his brother were taken,
but first they'd left the Douglas dead.

Who was the victor on that field
the Scots and the English won't agree;
but which force won as songs will tell it
matters little that I can see:

it surges on from year to year,
one more battle and still one more:
one in defence, one in aggression,
another to balance out the score.

*

Crows flap
fretting for blood.
The field of battle
is a ravening flood.

There is no safety
there is no shelter
the fell tide
will suck him under.

V

He did not fall at Otterburn;
he did not fall at Humbledowne;
he fell on the field at Shrewsbury,
a rebel against the crown.

He might have been a king himself;
he put one king upon the throne,
then turned against him, and sought to make
a king of my brother's son.

Families undo families;
kings go up and kings go down.
My man fell; but they propped him up
dead in Shrewsbury Town.

They tied his corpse in the marketplace,
jammed for their jeers between two stones;
then hacked him apart: a heavy price
he paid for juggling with thrones.

Four fair cities received his limbs,
far apart as the four winds are,
and his head stared north from the walls of York
fixed on Micklegate Bar.

*

Now let forgetfulness wash over
his bones and the land's bones,
the long snaky spine of the wall,
earthworks and standing stones,
rock and castle and tower and all.

*

There is no safety
there is no shelter
the fell flood
has drawn him under.

Henry Percy, known as Hotspur, eldest son of the first Earl of Northumberland, was born on 20 May 1364. The Percies were of Norman descent; they controlled the north of England with something like kingly power for several centuries, first as feudal lords and then as Barons of Alnwick and later Earls of Northumberland. They have been described as 'the hereditary guardians of the north and the scourge of Scotland'.

Accounts of Hotspur's life appear in the *Dictionary of National Biography* and the *Complete Peerage* and, in a fictionalised form, in Shakespeare's *Richard II* and *Henry IV, Part I*. He was a valiant and precocious warrior, and soon became a favourite with the people. He held such positions as were consistent with his rank and descent – Governor of Berwick and Warden of the Marches – but his chief pleasures were warfare (against the Scots or the French or anyone else) and, as an incidental sideline to this, political intrigue. It proved his undoing. He was killed at the Battle of Shrewsbury on 12 July 1403 in an unsuccessful rebellion against Henry IV, whom he had conspired to put on the throne.

His character was not entirely admirable, to modern eyes: he had a tendency to change sides and to choose his allies according to their usefulness, disregarding former loyalties; and he was as brutal as any of his opponents when he chose: his fate of being quartered after his death was one which he had himself ordered to be performed on a defeated enemy. However, his personal courage and his even then slightly anachronistic devotion to the ideals of chivalry made him a natural focus for the legends which have clung to his name.

The ballad is sung in the person of his wife Elizabeth Mortimer (not Kate, as Shakespeare calls her). She was born at Usk on 12 February 1371 and was the daughter of the Earl of March and the granddaughter, through her mother, of Edward III. She married Hotspur in 1379 and they had a daughter (whose date of birth is not recorded) and a son, born in 1393 and named after his father.

### I

*A halting spate*: Hotspur was said to have some kind of impediment in his speech, which at times delayed his fiery utterances.

*High is his prowess*: This section quotes the traditional elements of the ideal of chivalry.

### II

*Castle Leazes*: The pasture-lands north of the city wall.

*'Sir, I shall bear this token off...'*: The two speeches are taken from the version quoted by Froissart.

**IV**

*Otterburn*: The battle was probably fought on the night of 19 August 1388, by moonlight.

*Silver crescent*: This was the cap-badge of the Percies; their coat of arms bore a blue lion rampant.

*His brother*: Ralph Percy.

**V**

*Humbledowne* (or Humbleton, or Homildon Hill): The battle fought here on 13 September 1402 was Hotspur's revenge for Otterburn. The English won, capturing the 3rd Earl of Douglas (Archibald, successor to James, the 2nd Earl, who fell at Otterburn) and many other Scots.

*He might have been a king himself*: Not by legal succession; but if Elizabeth's nephew, the young Earl of March, had been set on the throne, Hotspur would very probably have been regent. In any case his popularity was such that the people could well have seen him as a possible king.

*Four fair cities*: After his body had been displayed in the marketplace at Shrewsbury it was buried; but a rumour arose that he was still alive, and his corpse was therefore disinterred and dismembered, and the four limbs sent to London, Bristol, Chester and Newcastle to be shown as evidence of his death.

# THE INCIDENT BOOK

(1986)

# Uniunea Scriitorilor

Caterpillars are falling on the Writers' Union.
The writers are indifferent to the caterpillars.
They sit over their wine at the metal tables
wearing animated expressions and eating fried eggs
with pickled gherkins, or (the dish of the day),
extremely small sausages: two each.

Meanwhile here and there an inch of grey bristles,
a miniature bottle-brush, twitches along a sleeve
or clings to a shoulder. The stone-paved courtyard
is dappled with desperate clumps of whiskers,
launched from the sunlit mulberry trees
to take their chance among literary furniture.

A poet ignores a fluffy intruder
in his bread-basket (the bread's all finished)
but flicks another from the velvet hat
(which surely she must have designed herself –
such elegance never appears in the shop-windows)
of his pretty companion, who looks like an actress.

The writers are talking more and more rapidly.
Not all are writers. One is a painter;
many are translators. Even those who are not
are adaptable and resourceful linguists.
'Pardon!' says one to the foreign visitor.
'Permit me! You have a worm on your back.'

# Leaving the Tate

Coming out with your clutch of postcards
in a Tate Gallery bag and another clutch
of images packed into your head you pause
on the steps to look across the river

and there's a new one: light bright buildings,
a streak of brown water, and such a sky
you wonder who painted it – Constable? No:
too brilliant. Crome? No: too ecstatic –

a madly pure Pre-Raphaelite sky,
perhaps, sheer blue apart from the white plumes
rushing up it (today, that is,
April. Another day would be different

but it wouldn't matter. All skies work.)
Cut to the lower right for a detail:
seagulls pecking on mud, below
two office blocks and a Georgian terrace.

Now swing to the left, and take in plane trees
bobbled with seeds, and that brick building,
and a red bus... Cut it off just there,
by the lamp-post. Leave the scaffolding in.

That's your next one. Curious how
these outdoor pictures didn't exist
before you'd looked at the indoor pictures,
the ones on the walls. But here they are now,

marching out of their panorama
and queuing up for the viewfinder
your eye's become. You can isolate them
by holding your optic muscles still.

You can zoom in on figure studies
(that boy with the rucksack), or still lives,
abstracts, townscapes. No one made them.
The light painted them. You're in charge

of the hanging committee. Put what space
you like around the ones you fix on,
and gloat. Art multiplies itself.
Art's whatever you choose to frame.


## The Bedroom Window


A small dazzle of stained glass which
I did not choose but might have, hanging
in front of the branches of a pine tree
which I do not own but covet; beyond them
a view of crinkly hills which I do not
etc and did not etc but might have
in another life, or the same life earlier.

The cat is fed, the plants are watered,
the milkman will call; the pine tree smells like
childhood. I am pretending to live here.
Out beyond the coloured glass and
the window-glass and the gully tall with
pine trees I dive back to wherever
I got my appetite for hills from.


## The Chiffonier


You're glad I like the chiffonier. But I
feel suddenly uneasy, scenting why
you're pleased I like this pretty thing you've bought,
the twin of one that stood beside your cot
when you were small: you've marked it down for me;
it's not too heavy to be sent by sea
when the time comes, and it's got space inside
to pack some other things you've set aside,
things that are small enough to go by water
twelve thousand miles to me, your English daughter.
I know your habits – writing all our names
in books and on the backs of picture-frames,
allotting antique glass and porcelain dishes
to granddaughters according to their wishes,
promising me the tinted photograph
of my great-grandmother. We used to laugh,
seeing how each occasional acquisition
was less for you than for later disposition:
'You know how Marilyn likes blue and white
china? I've seen some plates I thought I might
indulge in.' Bless you, Mother! But we're not
quite so inclined to laugh now that you've got
something that's new to you but not a part
of your estate: that weakness in your heart.
It makes my distance from you, when I go
back home next week, suddenly swell and grow
from thirty hours' flying to a vast
galactic space between present and past.
How many more times can I hope to come
to Wellington and find you still at home?
We've talked about it, as one has to, trying
to see the lighter aspects of your dying:

'You've got another twenty years or more,'
I said, 'but when you think you're at death's door
just let me know. I'll come and hang about
for however long it takes to see you out.'
'I don't think it'll be like that,' you said:
'I'll pop off suddenly one night in bed.'
How secretive! How satisfying! You'll
sneak off, a kid running away from school –
well, that at least's the only way I find
I can bring myself to see it in my mind.
But now I see you in your Indian skirt
and casual cornflower-blue linen shirt
in the garden, under your feijoa tree,
looking about as old or young as me.
Dear little Mother! Naturally I'm glad
you found a piece of furniture that had
happy associations with your youth;
and yes, I do admire it – that's the truth:
its polished wood and touch of Art Nouveau
appeal to me. But surely you must know
I value this or any other treasure
of yours chiefly because it gives you pleasure.
I have to write this now, while you're still here:
I want my mother, not her chiffonier.


## Tadpoles

*(for Oliver)*


Their little black thread legs, their threads of arms,
their mini-miniature shoulders, elbows, knees –
this piquant angularity, delicious
after that rippling smoothness, after nothing
but a flow of curves and roundnesses in water;
and their little hands, the size of their hands, the fingers
like hair-stubble, and their clumps-of-eyelashes feet…

Taddies, accept me as your grandmother,
a hugely gloating grand-maternal frog,
almost as entranced by other people's
tadpoles as I once was by my own,
that year when Oliver was still a tadpole
in Elizabeth's womb, and I a grandmother
only prospectively, and at long distance.


159

All this glory from globes of slithery glup!
Well, slithery glup was all right, with its cloudy
compacted spheres, its polka dots of blackness.
Then dots evolved into commas; the commas hatched.
When they were nothing but animated match-heads
with tails, a flickering flock of magnified
spermatazoa, they were already my darlings.

And Oliver lay lodged in his dreamy sphere,
a pink tadpole, a promise of limbs and language,
while my avatars of infancy grew up
into ribbon-tailed blackcurrants, fluttery-smooth,
and then into soaked brown raisins, a little venous,
with touches of transparency at the sides
where limbs minutely hinted at themselves.

It is the transformation that enchants.
As a mother reads her child's form in the womb,
imaging eyes and fingers, radar-sensing
a thumb in a blind mouth, so tadpole-watchers
can stare at the cunning shapes beneath the skin
and await the tiny, magnificent effloration.
It is a lesson for a grandmother.

My tadpoles grew to frogs in their generation;
they may have been the grandparents of these
about-to-be frogs. And Oliver's a boy,
hopping and bouncing in his bright green tracksuit,
my true darling; but too far away now
for me to call him across the world and say
'Oliver, look at what's happening to the tadpoles!'

# For Heidi with Blue Hair

When you dyed your hair blue
(or, at least, ultramarine
for the clipped sides, with a crest
of jet-black spikes on top)
you were sent home from school

because, as the headmistress put it,
although dyed hair was not
specifically forbidden, yours
was, apart from anything else,
not done in the school colours.

Tears in the kitchen, telephone calls
to school from your freedom-loving father:
'She's not a punk in her behaviour;
it's just a style.' (You wiped your eyes,
also not in a school colour.)

'She discussed it with me first –
we checked the rules.' 'And anyway, Dad,
it cost twenty-five dollars.
Tell them it won't wash out –
not even if I wanted to try.'

It would have been unfair to mention
your mother's death, but that
shimmered behind the arguments.
The school had nothing else against you;
the teachers twittered and gave in.

Next day your black friend had hers done
in grey, white and flaxen yellow –
the school colours precisely:
an act of solidarity, a witty
tease. The battle was already won.

# The Keepsake

*(in memory of Pete Laver)*


'To Fleur from Pete, on loan perpetual.'
It's written on the flyleaf of the book
I wouldn't let you give away outright:
'Just make it permanent loan,' I said – a joke
between librarians, professional
jargon. It seemed quite witty, on a night

when most things passed for wit. We were all hoarse
by then, from laughing at the bits you'd read
aloud – the heaving bosoms, blushing sighs,
demoniac lips. 'Listen to this!' you said:
' "Thus rendered bold by frequent intercourse
I dared to take her hand." ' We wiped our eyes.

' "Colonel, what mean these stains upon your dress?" '
We howled. And then there was Lord Ravenstone
faced with Augusta's dutiful rejection
in anguished prose; or, for a change of tone,
a touch of Gothic: Madame la Comtesse
's walled-up lover. An inspired collection:

*The Keepsake*, 1835; the standard
drawing-room annual, useful as a means
for luring ladies into chaste flirtation
in early 19th century courtship scenes.
I'd never seen a copy; often wondered.
Well, here it was – a pretty compilation

of tales and verses: stanzas by Lord Blank
and Countess This and Mrs That; demure
engravings, all white shoulders, corkscrew hair
and swelling bosoms; stories full of pure
sentiments, in which gentlemen of rank
urged suits upon the nobly-minded fair.

You passed the volume round, and poured more wine.
Outside your cottage lightning flashed again:
a Grasmere storm, theatrically right
for stories of romance and terror. Then
somehow, quite suddenly, the book was mine.
The date in it's five weeks ago tonight.

'On loan perpetual.' If that implied
some dark finality, some hint of 'nox
perpetua', something desolate and bleak,
we didn't see it then, among the jokes.
Yesterday, walking on the fells, you died.
I'm left with this, a trifling, quaint antique.

You'll not reclaim it now; it's mine to keep:
a keepsake, nothing more. You've changed the 'loan
perpetual' to a bequest by dying.
Augusta, Lady Blanche, Lord Ravenstone –
I've read the lot, trying to get to sleep.
The jokes have all gone flat. I can't stop crying.

## England's Glory

Red-tipped, explosive, self-complete:
one you can strike on the coal-face, or
the sole of your boot. Not for the south, where
soft men with soft hands rub effete
brown-capped sticks on a toning strip
chequered with coffee-grounds, the only
match for the matches, and any lonely
stray (if they let them stray) picked up
from a table or found loose in a pocket
can't, without its container, flare
fire at a stroke: is not a pure-
ly self-contained ignition unit.

'Security' proclaims the craven
yellow box with its Noah's ark,
'Brymay' Special Safety's trade-mark
for southern consumption. That's all right, then:
bankers can take them home to Surrey
for their cigars, and scatter the odd
match-head, whether or not it's dead,
on their parquet floors, without the worry
of subsequent arson. Not like here
where a match is a man's match, an object
to be handled with as much respect
but as casually as a man's beer.

You can't mistake the England's Glory
box: its crimson, blue and white
front's a miniature banner, fit
for the Durham Miners' Gala, gaudy
enough to march ahead of a band.
Forget that placid ark: the vessel
this one's adorned with has two funnels
gushing fat blue smoke to the wind.
The side's of sandpaper. The back
label's functional, printed with either
holiday vouchers, a special offer
on World Cup tickets, or this month's joke.

Somewhere across England's broad
midriff, wanderingly drawn
from west to east, there exists a line
to the north of which the shops provide
(catering for a sudden switch
of taste) superior fried fish, runnier
yogurt, blouses cut for the fuller
northern figure; and the northern match.
Here England's Glory begins; through all
the vigorous north it reigns unrivalled
until its truce with Scottish Bluebell
round about Berwick and Carlisle.

## The Genius of Surrey

The landscape of my middle childhood
lacked factories. There had been no
industrial revolution in Surrey,
was the message. Woods and shops and houses,
churches, allotments, pubs and schools
and loonie-bins were all we had.

Except, of course, the sewerage works,
on 'Surridge Hill', as we used to call it.
How sweetly rural the name sounds!
Wordsworth's genius, said Walter Pater,
would have found its true test
had he become the poet of Surrey.

164

Yorkshire had a talent for mills
and placed them to set off its contours;
Westmorland could also have worn
a few more factories with an air.
As for Surrey's genius, that
was found to be for the suburban.


## Loving Hitler


There they were around the wireless
waiting to listen to Lord Haw-Haw.
'Quiet now, children!' they said as usual:
'Ssh, be quiet! We're trying to listen.'
'Germany calling!' said Lord Haw-Haw.

I came out with it: 'I love Hitler.'
They turned on me: 'You can't love *Hitler*!
Dreadful, wicked –' (mutter, mutter,
the shocked voices buzzing together) –
'Don't be silly. You don't mean it.'

I held out for perhaps five minutes,
a mini-proto-neo-Nazi,
six years old and wanting attention.
Hitler always got their attention;
now I had it, for five minutes.

Everyone at school loved someone,
and it had to be a boy or a man
if you were a girl. So why not Hitler?
Of course, you couldn't love Lord Haw-Haw;
but Hitler – well, he was so famous!

It might be easier to love Albert,
the boy who came to help with the milking,
but Albert laughed at me. Hitler wouldn't:
one thing you could say for Hitler,
you never heard him laugh at people.

All the same, I settled for Albert.

*Schools*

## Halfway Street, Sidcup

'We did sums at school, Mummy –
you do them like this: look.' I showed her.

It turned out she knew already.


## St Gertrude's, Sidcup

Nuns, now: ladies in black hoods
for teachers – surely that was surprising?

It seems not. It was just England:
like houses made of brick, with stairs,

and dark skies, and Christmas coming
in winter, and there being a war on.

I was five, and unsurprisable –
except by nasty dogs, or the time

when I ran to catch the bus from school
and my knickers fell down in the snow.


## Scalford School

The French boy was sick on the floor at prayers.
For years his name made me feel sick too:
Maurice. The teachers said it the English way,
but he was French, or French-speaking –
Belgian, perhaps; at any rate from some
country where things were wrong in 1940.
Until I grew up, 'Maurice' meant
his narrow pale face, pointed chin,
bony legs, and the wet pink sick.

But we were foreign too, of course,
my sister and I, in spite of our
unthinkingly acquired Leicestershire accents.
An older girl was struck one day
by our, to us, quite ordinary noses;
made an anthropological deduction:
'Have all the other people in New Zealand
got silly little noses too?'
I couldn't remember. Firmly I said 'Yes.'


## Salfords, Surrey


Forget about the school – there was one,
which I've near enough forgotten.

But look at this – and you still can,
on the corner of Honeycrock Lane –

this tiny tin-roofed shed of brick,
once the smallest possible Public

Library. I used to lie
flat on the floor, and work my way

along the shelves, trying to choose
between Rose Fyleman's fairy verse

and *Tales of Sir Benjamin Bulbous, Bart.*
The book that really stuck in my heart

I can't identify: a saga
about a talking horse, the Pooka,

and Kathleen, and the quest they both
made through tunnels under the earth

for – something. Herbs and flowers came
into it, spangled through a dream

of eyebright, speedwell, Kathleen's bare
legs blotched blue with cold. Well; there

were other stories. When I'd read
all mine I'd see what Mummy had.

*Of Mice and Men*: that sounded nice.
I'd just got far enough to notice

it wasn't much like *Peter Rabbit*
when she took it away and hid it.

No loss, I'd say. But where shall I find
the Pooka's travels underground?


## Outwood


Milkmaids, buttercups, ox-eye daisies,
white and yellow in the tall grass:
I fought my way to school through flowers –
bird's-foot trefoil, clover, vetch –
my sandals all smudged with pollen,
seedy grass-heads caught in my socks.

At school I used to read, mostly,
and hide in the shed at dinnertime,
writing poems in my notebook.
'Little fairies dancing,' I wrote,
and 'Peter and I, we watch the birds fly,
high in the sky, in the evening.'

Then home across the warm common
to tease my little sister again:
'I suppose you thought I'd been to school:
I've been to work in a bicycle shop.'
Mummy went to a real job
every day, on a real bicycle;

Doris used to look after us.
She took us for a walk with a soldier,
through the damp ferns in the wood
into a clearing like a garden,
rosy-pink with beds of campion,
herb-robert, lady's smock.

The blackberry briars were pale with blossom.
I snagged my tussore dress on a thorn;
Doris didn't even notice.
She and the soldier lay on the grass;
he leaned over her pink blouse
and their voices went soft and round, like petals.

## On the School Bus

The little girls in the velvet collars
(twins, we thought) had lost their mother:
the ambulance men had had to scrape her
off the road, said the sickening whispers.

Horror's catching. The safe procedure
to ward it off, or so we gathered,
was a homeopathic dose of torture.
So we pulled their hair, like all the others.

## Earlswood

Air-raid shelters at school were damp tunnels
where you sang 'Ten Green Bottles' yet again
and might as well have been doing decimals.

At home, though, it was cosier and more fun:
cocoa and toast inside the Table Shelter,
our iron-panelled bunker, our new den.

By day we ate off it; at night you'd find us
under it, the floor plump with mattresses
and the wire grilles neatly latched around us.

You had to be careful not to bump your head;
we padded the hard metal bits with pillows,
then giggled in our glorious social bed.

What could be safer? What could be more romantic
than playing cards by torchlight in a raid?
Odd that it made our mother so neurotic

169

to hear the sirens; we were quite content —
but slightly cramped once there were four of us,
after we'd taken in old Mrs Brent

from down by the Nag's Head, who'd been bombed out.
She had her arm in plaster, but she managed
to dress herself, and smiled, and seemed all right.

Perhaps I just imagined hearing her
moaning a little in the night, and shaking
splinters of glass out of her long grey hair.

The next week we were sent to Leicestershire.


## Scalford Again

Being in Mr Wood's class this time,
and understanding, when he explained it clearly,
about the outside of a bicycle wheel
travelling around faster than the centre;
and not minding his warts; and liking Scripture
because of the Psalms: I basked in all this
no less than in the Infants the time before,
with tambourines and Milly-Molly-Mandy.
Although I'd enjoyed Milly-Molly-Mandy:
it had something to do with apricots, I thought,
or marigolds; or some warm orange glow.


## Neston

Just visiting: another village school
with a desk for me to fill, while Chippenham
decided whether it wanted me — too young
for there, too over-qualified for here.

I knew it all — except, of course, geography.
Here was a map; I vaguely scratched in towns.
Ah, but here was a job: the infant teacher
was called away for half an hour. Would I...?

Marooned there in a tide of little bodies
alive with Wiltshire voices, I was dumb.
They skipped about my feet, a flock of lambs
bleating around a daft young heifer.


## Chippenham


The maths master was eight feet tall.
He jabbed his clothes-prop arm at me
halfway across the classroom, stretched
his knobbly finger, shouted 'You!

You're only here one day in three,
and when you are you might as well
not be, for all the work you do!
What do you think you're playing at?'

What did I think? I shrank into
my grubby blouse. Who did I think
I was, among these blazered boys,
these tidy girls in olive serge?

My green skirt wasn't uniform:
clothes were on coupons, after all.
I'd get a gymslip – blue, not green –
for Redhill Grammar, some time soon

when we went home. But, just for now,
what did I think? I thought I was
betrayed. I thought of how I'd stood
an hour waiting for the bus

that morning, by a flooded field,
watching the grass-blades drift and sway
beneath the water like wet hair;
hoping for Mrs Johnson's call:

'Jean, are you there? The clock was wrong.
You've missed the bus.' And back I'd run
to change my clothes, be Jean again,
play with the baby, carry pails

of water from the village tap,
go to the shop, eat toast and jam,
and then, if she could shake enough
pennies and farthings from her bag,

we might get to the pictures. But
the clock was fast, it seemed, not slow;
the bus arrived; and as I slid
anonymously into it

an elegant male prefect said
'Let Fleur sit down, she's got bad feet.'
I felt my impetigo scabs
blaze through my shoes. How did he know?


## Tunbridge Wells


My turn for Audrey Pomegranate,
all-purpose friend for newcomers;
the rest had had enough of her –
her too-much hair, her too-much flesh,
her moles, her sideways-gliding mouth,
her smirking knowledge about rabbits.

Better a gluey friend than none,
and who was I to pick and choose?
She nearly stuck; but just in time
I met a girl called Mary Button,
a neat Dutch doll as clean as soap,
and Audrey P. was back on offer.

## The High Tree

There was a tree higher than clouds or lightning,
higher than any plane could fly.

England huddled under its roots; leaves from it
fluttered on Europe out of the sky.

The weather missed it: it was higher than weather,
up in the sunshine, always dry.

It was a refuge. When you sat in its branches
threatening strangers passed you by.

Nothing could find you. Even friendly people,
if you invited them to try,

couldn't climb very far. It made them dizzy:
they'd shiver and shut their eyes and cry,

and you'd have to guide them down again, backwards,
wishing they hadn't climbed so high.

So it wasn't a social tree. It was perfect
for someone solitary and shy

who liked gazing out over miles of history,
watching it happen, like a spy,

and was casual about heights, but didn't fancy
coming down again to defy

the powers below. Odd that they didn't notice
all this climbing on the sly,

and odder still, if they knew, that they didn't ban it.
Knowing them now, you'd wonder why.

## Drowning

'*Si qua mulier maritum suum, cui legitime est iuncta, dimiserit, necetur in luto.*'
[*If any woman has killed her lawfully married husband let her be drowned in mud.*]
LEX BURGUND., 34, I.


Death by drowning drowns the soul:
bubbles cannot carry it;
frail pops of air, farts
loosed in water are no vessels
for the immortal part of us.
And in a pit of mud, what bubbles?
There she lies, her last breath with her,
her soul rotting in her breast.

\*

Is the sea better, then?
Will the salty brine preserve
pickled souls for the Day of Judgement?
Are we herrings to be trawled
in long nets by Saint Peter?
Ocean is a heavy load:
*My soul flies up to thee, O God –*
but not through mud, not through water.

And so, Bishop Synesius,
how can you wonder that we stand
with drawn swords on this bucking deck,
choosing to fall on friendly steel
and squirt our souls into the heavens
rather than choke them fathoms deep?
One more lash of the storm and it's done:
self-murder, but not soul-murder.

Then let the fishes feast on us
and slurp our blood after we're finished:
they'll find no souls to suck from us.
Yours, perhaps, has a safe-conduct:
you're a bishop, and subtle, and Greek.
Well, sir, pray and ponder. But our
language has no word for dilemma.
Drowning's the strongest word for death.

## 'Personal Poem'

It's the old story of the personal;
or of the Person – 'Al', we could call him –
with his oneness, his centrality,
fingers tapping to the band music,
and his eyes glowing like that
as if he had invented the guitar;
or coming around the corner on his tractor
calling out some comment you just missed.

The radios begin at 6 a.m.
It is really a very crowded city.
You're lucky to find two rooms, one for sleeping,
and a patch of allotment for potatoes.

Here we are on the hills, and it's no better.
Of course the birds are singing, but they would.
All you get is contempt, didn't they say so?
All right, contemn us.
We asked for nothing but a few gestures –
that kiss inside his open collar,
between the neck and shoulder, shockingly
personal to watch.

It's Al again, laughing in his teeth,
telling us about his Jamaican childhood
and the time his friend had crabs
from making love to the teacher's maid.
'It gave me a funny feeling,' he says
'to see them crawling there, little animals.
I hadn't even grown hair on mine.
In a way I was jealous –
imagine!' We imagine.

All these people running about in tracksuits
for nothing. And one standing at the gate
with a paper bag of bananas. 'Hi,' he says,
'How are you?' Nobody answers.

So at the May Day rally there they are.
Surely that's his jacket she's wearing?
And the face under the hair is his,
the way she wrinkles her nose.
How people give themselves away!
Yet all we have is hearsay.

Too late to take a boat out;
and anyway, the lake's crowded,
kids and oars together, and all their voices.
But really no one in particular,
unless you say so. Unless we say so.

## An Epitaph

I wish to apologise for being mangled.
It was the romantic temperament
that did for me. I could stand rejection –
so grand, 'the stone the builders rejected...' –
but not acceptance. 'Alas,' I said
(a word I use), 'alas, I am taken
up, or in, or out of myself:
shall I never be solitary?'
Acceptance fell on me like a sandbag.
My bones crack. It squelches out of them.
Ah, acceptance! Leave me under this stone.

## Being Taken from the Place

Less like an aircraft than a kettle,
this van, the way the floor buzzes
tinnily over its boiling wheels,
rolling me south.
                    Sounds flick backwards
in a travelling cauldron of noise. I lie
on the metal floor, hearing their voices
whirring like mechanical flies
over the seething burr of the engine.

They won't hear if I talk to myself;
whatever I say they can't hear me.
I say 'Illness is a kind of failure.'
I say 'Northumbrian rose quartz.'

# Accidents

The accidents are never happening:
they are too imaginable to be true.
The driver knows his car is still on the road,
heading for Durham in the rain.
The mother knows her baby is just asleep,
curled up with his cuddly blanket, waiting
to be lifted and fed: there's no such thing as cot-death.
The rescue party digging all night in the dunes
can't believe the tunnel has really collapsed:
the children have somehow gone to their Auntie's house;
she has lent them their cousins' pyjamas, they are sitting
giggling together in the big spare room,
pretending to try and spill each other's cocoa.

# On the Land

I'm still too young to remember how
I learned to mind a team of horses,
to plough and harrow: not a knack
you'd lose easily, once you had it.

It was in the Great War, that much
remembered age. I was a landgirl
in my puttees and boots and breeches
and a round hat like a felt halo.

We didn't mind the lads laughing:
let them while they could, we thought,
they hadn't long. But it seemed long –
hay-making, and apple-picking,

and storing all those scented things
in sneezy dimness in the barn.
Then Jack turned seventeen and went,
and I knew Ted would go soon.

He went the week of Candlemas.
After that it was all weather:
frosts and rains and spring and summer,
and the long days growing longer.

It rained for the potato harvest.
The front of my smock hung heavy
with claggy mud, from kneeling in it
mining for strays. Round segments

chopped clean off by the blade
flashed white as severed kneecaps.
I grubbed for whole ones, baby skulls
to fill my sack again and again.

When the pain came, it wouldn't
stop. I couldn't stand. I dropped
the sack and sank into a trench.
Ethel found me doubled up.

Mr Gregson took me home,
jolting on the back of the wagon.
I tossed and writhed on my hard bed,
my head hunched into the bolster,

dreaming of how if just for once,
for half an hour, the knobbly mattress
could turn into a billow of clouds
I might be able to get to sleep.


## Icon


In the interests of economy
I am not going to tell you
what happened between the time
when they checked into the hotel

with its acres of tiled bathrooms
(but the bidet in theirs was cracked)
and the morning two days later
when he awoke to find her gone.

After he had read her note
and done the brief things he could do
he found himself crossing the square
to the Orthodox Cathedral.

The dark icon by the door
was patched with lumpy silver islands
nailed to the Virgin's robes; they looked
like flattened-out Monopoly tokens,

he thought: a boot, and something like
a heart, and a pair of wings, and something
oblong. They were hard to see
in the brown light, but he peered at them

for several minutes, leaning over
the scarved head of an old woman
on her knees there, blocking his view;
who prayed and prayed and wouldn't move.


## Drawings

The ones not in the catalogue:
little sketches, done in her garden – this
head of a child (the same child
we saw in the picnic scene, remember?)
And trees, of course, and grasses,
and a study of hawthorn berries.
Doodles, unfinished drafts: look
at this chestnut leaf, abandoned in mid-
stroke – a telephone-call, perhaps;
a visitor; some interruption.

She may have been happier,
or happy longer, or at least more often…
but that's presumption. Let's move on:
grasses again; a group of stones
from her rockery, done in charcoal; and this
not quite completed pencil sketch of
a tiger lily, the springy crown
of petals curved back on itself
right to the stem, the long electric
stamens almost still vibrating.


## The Telephone Call

They asked me 'Are you sitting down?
Right? This is Universal Lotteries,'
they said. 'You've won the top prize,
the Ultra-super Global Special.
What would you do with a million pounds?

Or, actually, with more than a million –
not that it makes a lot of difference
once you're a millionaire.' And they laughed.

'Are you OK?' they asked – 'Still there?
Come on, now, tell us, how does it feel?'
I said 'I just …I can't believe it!'
They said 'That's what they all say.
What else? Go on, tell us about it.'
I said 'I feel the top of my head
has floated off, out through the window,
revolving like a flying saucer.'

'That's unusual,' they said. 'Go on.'
I said 'I'm finding it hard to talk.
My throat's gone dry, my nose is tingling.
I think I'm going to sneeze – or cry.'
'That's right,' they said, 'don't be ashamed
of giving way to your emotions.
It isn't every day you hear
you're going to get a million pounds.

Relax, now, have a little cry;
we'll give you a moment…' 'Hang on!' I said.
'I haven't bought a lottery ticket
for years and years. And what did you say
the company's called?' They laughed again.
'Not to worry about a ticket.
We're Universal. We operate
a Retrospective Chances Module.

Nearly everyone's bought a ticket
in some lottery or another,
once at least. We buy up the files,
feed the names into our computer,
and see who the lucky person is.'
'Well, that's incredible,' I said.
'It's marvellous. I still can't quite…
I'll believe it when I see the cheque.'

'Oh,' they said, 'there's no cheque.'
'But the money?' 'We don't deal in money.
Experiences are what we deal in.
You've had a great experience, right?
Exciting? Something you'll remember?
That's your prize. So congratulations
from all of us at Universal.
Have a nice day!' And the line went dead.

*Incidentals*

## Excavations

Here is a hole full of men shouting
'I don't love you. I loved you once
but I don't now. I went off you,
or I was frightened, or my wife was pregnant,
or I found I preferred men instead.'

What can I say to that kind of talk?
'Thank you for being honest, you
who were so shifty when it happened,
pretending you were suddenly busy
with your new job or your new conscience.'

I chuck them a shovelful of earth
to make them blink for a bit, to smirch
their green eyes and their long lashes
or their brown eyes... Pretty bastards:
the rain will wash their bawling faces

and I bear them little enough ill will.
Now on to the next hole,
covered and fairly well stamped down,
full of the men whom I stopped loving
and didn't always tell at the time –

being, I found, rather busy
with my new man or my new freedom.
These are quiet and unaccusing,
cuddled up with their subsequent ladies,
hardly unsettling the bumpy ground.

## Pastoral

Eat their own hair, sheep do,
nibbling away under the snow, under their bellies –
calling it wool makes it no more palatable.

What else is there to do in the big drifts,
forced against a wall of wet stone?
But let me have your hair to nibble

before we are in winter; and the thong
of dark seeds you wear at your neck;
and for my tongue the salt on your skin to gobble.


## Kissing

The young are walking on the riverbank,
arms around each other's waists and shoulders,
pretending to be looking at the waterlilies
and what might be a nest of some kind, over
there, which two who are clamped together
mouth to mouth have forgotten about.
The others, making courteous detours
around them, talk, stop talking, kiss.
They can see no one older than themselves.
It's their river. They've got all day.

Seeing's not everything. At this very
moment the middle-aged are kissing
in the backs of taxis, on the way
to airports and stations. Their mouths and tongues
are soft and powerful and as moist as ever.
Their hands are not inside each other's clothes
(because of the driver) but locked so tightly
together that it hurts: it may leave marks
on their not of course youthful skin, which they won't
notice. They too may have futures.

# Double-take

You see your nextdoor neighbour from above,
from an upstairs window, and he reminds you
of your ex-lover, who is bald on top,
which you had forgotten. At ground level
there is no resemblance. Next time you chat
with your nextdoor neighbour, you are relieved
to find that you don't fancy him.

A week later you meet your ex-lover
at a party, after more than a year.
He reminds you (although only slightly)
of your nextdoor neighbour. He has a paunch
like your neighbour's before he went on that diet.
You remember how much you despise him.

He behaves as if he's pleased to see you.
When you leave (a little earlier
than you'd intended, to get away)
he gives you a kiss which is more than neighbourly
and says he'll ring you. He seems to mean it.
How odd! But you are quite relieved
to find that you don't fancy him.

Unless you do? Or why that sudden
something, once you get outside
in the air? Why are your legs prancing
so cheerfully along the pavement?
And what exactly have you just remembered?
You go home cursing chemistry.

# Choices

There was never just one book for the desert island,
one perfectly tissue-typed aesthetic match,
that wouldn't drive you crazy within six months;
just as there was never one all-purpose
ideal outfit, unquestionably right
for wearing at the ball on the *Titanic*
and also in the lifeboat afterwards.

And never, *a fortiori*, just one man;
if it's not their conversation or their habits
(more irritating, even, than your own –
and who would you wish those on?) it's their bodies:
two-thirds of them get fatter by the minute,
the bony ones turn out to be psychopaths,
and the few in the middle range go bald.

Somehow you'll end up there, on the island,
in your old jeans and that comic dressing-gown
one of the fast-fatteners always laughed at,
with a blank notebook (all you've brought to read)
and a sea-and-sun-proof crate of cigarettes;
but with nobody, thank God, to lecture you
on how he managed to give them up.

## Street Scene, London N2

This is the front door. You can just see
the number on it, there behind the piano,
between the young man with the fierce expression
and the one with the axe, who's trying not to laugh.

Those furry-headed plants beside the step
are Michaelmas daisies, as perhaps you've guessed,
although they're not in colour; and the path
is tiled in red and black, like a Dutch interior.

But the photograph, of course, is black and white.
The piano also sported black and white
when it was whole (look, you can see its ribcage,
the wiry harp inside it, a spread wing).

The young men are playing Laurel and Hardy
(though both are tall, and neither of them is fat,
and one of them is actually a pianist):
they are committing a pianocide.

It wasn't really much of a piano:
warped and fungoid, grossly out of tune –
facts they have not imparted to the wincing
passers-by, whom you will have to imagine.

You will also have to imagine, if you dare,
the jangling chords of axe-blow, saw-stroke, screeching
timber, wires twanged in a terminal
appassionato. This is a silent picture.

Laurel and Hardy will complete their show:
the wires, released from their frame, will thrash and tangle
and be tamed into a ball; the varnished panels
will be sawn stacks of boards and blocks and kindling.

Later the mother will come home for Christmas.
The fire will purr and tinkle in the grate,
a chromatic harmony of tones; and somewhere
there'll be a muffled sack of snarling keys.

# Gentlemen's Hairdressers

The barbers' shop has gone anonymous:
white paint, glossy as Brilliantine
('The Perfect Hairdressing') has covered
Jim's and Alfred's friendly monickers.

GENTLEMENS HAIRD in chaste blue Roman
glorifies pure form. The man
on the ladder lays a scarlet slash
of marking-tape for the next upright.

Below him Jim and Alfred are still
in business. Alfred munches a pie
and dusts the crumbs from his grey moustache
over the racing-page. A gentleman

tilts his head under Jim's clippers.
In the window the Durex poster,
the one with the motorbike, has faded
to pale northern shades of sea.

An hour later the ladder's gone
and purity's been deposed: the lettering's
denser now, the Roman caps
blocked in with three-dimensional grey.

The word 'Styling' in shapeless cursive
wriggles above the open door.
Swaddled and perched on Alfred's chair
a tiny Greek boy squeals and squeals.

# Post Office

The queue's right out through the glass doors
to the street: Thursday, pension day.
They built this Post Office too small.
Of course, the previous one was smaller –
a tiny prefab, next to the betting-shop,
says the man who's just arrived;
and the present one, at which we're queuing,
was cherry trees in front of a church.
The church was where the supermarket is:
'My wife and I got married in that church,'
the man says. 'We hold hands sometimes
when we're standing waiting at the checkout –
have a little moment together!' He laughs.
The queue shuffles forward a step.
Three members of it silently vow
never to grow old in this suburb;
one vows never to grow old at all.
'I first met her over there,' the man says,
'on that corner where the bank is now.
The other corner was Williams Brothers –
remember Williams Brothers? They gave you tokens,
tin money, like, for your dividend.'
The woman in front of him remembers.
She nods, and swivels her loose lower denture,
remembering Williams Brothers' metal tokens,
and the marble slab on the cheese-counter,
and the carved mahogany booth where you went to pay.
The boy in front of her is chewing gum;
his jaws rotate with the same motion
as hers: to and fro, to and fro.

# Demonstration

'YOU ARE NOW WALKING IN THE ROAD.
The lines marked out with sticky tape
are where the kerb is going to be
under the traffic-scheme proposals.
This tree will go. The flower-beds
and seats outside the supermarket
will go. The pavements will be narrowed
to make room for six lanes of traffic.'

We are now walking in the road
with a few banners and some leaflets
and forms to sign for a petition.
The Council will ignore them all.
The Council wants a monster junction
with traffic-islands, metal railings,
computer-managed lights and crossings,
and lots and lots of lanes of traffic.

We are still walking in the road.
It seems a long time since we started,
and most of us are getting older
(the ones who aren't, of course, are dead).
This borough has the highest number
of pensioners in Greater London.
Perhaps the junction, with its modern
split-second lights, will cut them down.

But while we're walking in the road
others are driving. At our backs
we hear the roar of heavy traffic
churning from Finchley to Westminster;
and over it, from a loudspeaker,
a stern, conceited female voice
with artificial vowels exhorts us:
'Come with us into the nineties!'

# Witnesses

We three in our dark decent clothes,
unlike ourselves, more like the three
witches, we say, crouched over the only
ashtray, smoke floating into our hair,

wait. An hour; another hour.
If you stand up and walk ten steps
to the glass doors you can see her there
in the witness box, a Joan of Arc,

straight, still, her neck slender,
her lips moving from time to time
in reply to voices we can't hear:
'I put it to you... I should like to suggest...'

It's her small child who is at stake.
His future hangs from these black-clad
proceedings, these ferretings under her sober
dress, under our skirts and dresses

to sniff out corruption: 'I put it to you
that in fact your husband... that my client...
that you yourself initiated the violence...
that your hysteria...' She sits like marble.

We pace the corridors, peep at the distance
from door to witness box (two steps up,
remember, be careful not to trip
when the time comes) and imagine them there,

the ones we can't see. A man in a wig
and black robes. Two other men
in lesser wigs and gowns. More men
in dark suits. We sit down together,

shake the smoke from our hair, pass round
more cigarettes (to be held carefully
so as not to smirch our own meek versions
of their clothing), and wait to be called.

# Last Song

Goodbye, sweet symmetry. Goodbye, sweet world
of mirror-images and matching halves,
where animals have usually four legs
and people nearly always two;
where birds and bats and butterflies and bees
have balanced wings, and even flies
can fly straight if they try. Goodbye
to one-a-side for eyes and ears and arms
and breasts and balls and shoulder-blades
and hands; goodbye to the straight line
drawn down the central spine,
making us double in a world
where oddness is acceptable only
under the sea, for the lop-sided lobster,
the wonky oyster, the creepily rotated
flatfish with both eyes over one gill;
goodbye to the sweet certitudes of our
mammalian order, where to be
born with one eye or three thumbs
points to not being human. It will come.

In the next world, when this one's gone skew-whiff,
we shall be algae or lichen, things
we've hardly even needed to pronounce.
If the flounder still exists it will be king.

# TIME-ZONES

(1991)

# Counting

You count the fingers first: it's traditional.
(You assume the doctor counted them too,
when he lifted up the slimy surprise
with its long dark pointed head and its father's nose
at 2.13 a.m. – 'Look at the clock!'
said Sister: 'Remember the time: 2.13.')

Next day the head's turned pink and round;
the nose is a blob. You fumble under the gown
your mother embroidered with a sprig of daisies,
as she embroidered your own Viyella gowns
when you were a baby. You fish out
curly triangular feet. You count the toes.

'There's just one little thing,' says Sister:
'His ears – they don't quite match. One
has an extra whorl in it. No one will notice.'
You notice like mad. You keep on noticing.
Then you hear a rumour: a woman in the next ward
has had a stillbirth. Or was it something worse?

You lie there, bleeding gratefully.
You've won the Nobel Prize, and the VC,
and the State Lottery, and gone to heaven.
Feed-time comes. They bring your bundle –
the right one: it's him all right.
You count his eyelashes: the ideal number.

You take him home. He learns to walk.
From time to time you eye him,
nonchalantly, from each side.
He has an admirable nose.
No one ever notices his ears. No one
ever stands on both sides of him at once.

He grows up. He has beautiful children.

## Libya

When the Americans were bombing Libya
(that time when it looked as if this was it at last,
the match in the petrol-tank which will flare sooner or later,
and the whole lot was about to go up)

Gregory turned on the television during dinner
and Elizabeth asked the children to be quiet
because this was important, we needed to watch the news –
'It might be the beginning of the end,' she said.

Oliver, who was seven, said 'But I'm too young to die!'
Lily, who was five, said 'I don't want to die! I don't!'
Oliver said 'I know! Let's get under the table!'
Lily said, 'Yes, let's get under the table!'

So they got under the table, and wriggled around our legs
making the dishes rattle, and we didn't stop them
because we were busy straining to hear the news
and watching the fat bombers filling the screen.

It was a noisy ten minutes, one way and another.
Julia, who was fifteen months, chuckled in her high chair,
banging her spoon for her wonderful brother and sister,
and sang 'Three blind mice, three blind mice'.


## What May Happen

The worst thing that can happen –
to let the child go;
but you must not say so
or else it may happen.

The stranger looms in the way
holding an olive-twig.
The child's not very big;
he is beginning to cry.

How can you stand by?
A cloud crushes the hill.
Everything stands still.
Everything moves away.

The stranger is still a stranger
but the child is not your child.
Too soon, before he's old,
he may become a stranger.

He is his own child.
He has a way to go.
Others have lived it through:
watch, and turn cold.


## My Father


When I got up that morning I had no father.
I know that now. I didn't suspect it then.
They drove me through the tangle of Manchester
to the station, and I pointed to a sign:

'Hulme' it said – though all I saw was a rubbled
wasteland, a walled-off dereliction. 'Hulme –
that's where they lived,' I said, 'my father's people.
It's nowhere now.' I coughed in the traffic fumes.

Hulme and Medlock. A quarter of a mile
to nowhere, to the names of some nothing streets
beatified in my family history file,
addresses on birth and marriage certificates:

Back Clarence Street, Hulme; King Street (but which one?);
One-in-Four Court, Chorlton-upon-Medlock.
Meanwhile at home on my answering machine
a message from New Zealand: please ring back.

In his day it was factory smoke, not petrol,
that choked the air and wouldn't let him eat
until, the first day out from Liverpool,
sea air and toast unlocked his appetite.

He took up eating then, at the age of ten –
too late to cancel out the malnutrition
of years and generations. A small man,
though a tough one. He'll have needed a small coffin.

I didn't see it; he went to it so suddenly,
too soon, with both his daughters so far away:
a box of ashes in Karori Cemetery,
a waft of smoke in the clean Wellington sky.

Even from here it catches in my throat
as I puzzle over the Manchester street-plan,
checking the index, magnifying the net
of close-meshed streets in M2 and M1.

Not all the city's motorways and high-rise.
There must be roads that I can walk along
and know they walked there, even if their houses
have vanished like the cobble-stones – that throng

of Adcocks, Eggingtons, Joynsons, Lamberts, Listers.
I'll go to look for where they were born and bred.
I'll go next month; we'll both go, I and my sister.
We'll tell him about it, when he stops being dead.


## Cattle in Mist


A postcard from my father's childhood –
the one nobody photographed or painted;
the one we never had, my sister and I.
Such feeble daughters – couldn't milk a cow
(watched it now and then, but no one taught us).
How could we hold our heads up, having never
pressed them into the warm flank of a beast
and lured the milk down? Hiss, hiss, in a bucket:
routine, that's all. Not ours. That one missed us.

His later childhood, I should say;
not his second childhood – that he evaded
by dying – and his first was Manchester.
But out there in the bush, from the age of ten,
in charge of milking, rounding up the herd,
combing the misty fringes of the forest
(as he would have had to learn not to call it)
at dawn, and again after school, for stragglers;
cursing them; bailing them up; it was no childhood.


195

A talent-spotting teacher saved him.
The small neat smiling boy (I'm guessing)
evolved into a small neat professor.
He could have spent his life wreathed in cow-breath,
a slave to endlessly refilling udders,
companion of heifers, midwife at their calvings,
judicious pronouncer on milk-yields and mastitis,
survivor of the bull he bipped on the nose
('Tell us again, Daddy!') as it charged him.

All his cattle: I drive them back
into the mist, into the dawn haze
where they can look romantic; where they must
have wandered now for sixty or seventy years.
Off they go, then, tripping over the tree-roots,
pulling up short to lip at a tasty twig,
bumping into each other, stumbling off again
into the bush. He never much liked them.
He'll never need to rustle them back again.


## Toads


Let's be clear about this: I love toads.

So when I found our old one dying,
washed into the drain by flood-water
in the night and then – if I can bring myself
to say it – scalded by soapy lather
I myself had let out of the sink,
we suffered it through together.

It was the summer of my father's death.
I saw his spirit in every visiting creature,
in every small thing at risk of harm:
bird, moth, butterfly, beetle,
the black rabbit lolloping along concrete,
lost in suburbia; and our toad.

If we'd seen it once a year that was often,
but the honour of being chosen by it
puffed us up: a toad of our own
trusting us not to hurt it
when we had to lift it out of its den
to let the plumber get at the water-main.

And now this desperate damage: the squat
compactness unhinged, made powerless.
Dark, straight, its legs extended,
flippers paralysed, it lay lengthwise
flabby-skinned across my palm,
cold and stiff as the Devil's penis.

I laid it on soil; the shoulders managed
a few slow twitches, pulled it an inch forward.
But the blowflies knew: they called it dead
and stippled its back with rays of pearly stitching.
Into the leaves with it then, poor toad,
somewhere cool, where I can't watch it.

Perhaps it was very old? Perhaps it was ready?
Small comfort, through ten guilt-ridden days.
And then, one moist midnight, out in the country,
a little shadow shaped like a brown leaf
hopped out of greener leaves and came to me.
Twice I had to lift it from my doorway:

a gently throbbing handful – calm, comely,
its feet tickling my palm like soft bees.

## Under the Lawn

It's hard to stay angry with a buttercup
threading through the turf (less and less a lawn
with each jagging rip of the fork or scoop
of the trowel) but a dandelion can

inspire righteous fury: that taproot
drilling down to where it's impossible
ever quite to reach (although if it's cut
through that's merely a minor check) until

clunk: what's this? And it's spade-time. Several hours
later, eleven slabs of paving-stone
(submerged so long ago that the neighbours
who've been on the watch since 1941

'never remember seeing a path there') with,
lying marooned singly on three of them,
an octagonal threepence, a George the Fifth
penny and, vaguely missed from their last home

for fifteen years or so and rusted solid,
Grandpa's scissors, the ones for hairdressing
from his barbering days: plain steel, not plated;
still elegant; the tip of one blade still missing.


## Wren Song


How can I prove to you
that we've got wrens in the garden?

A quick flick of a tail
in or out of the ivy hedge
is all you'll ever see of them;

and anyway, I'm asleep.
Not dreaming, though: I can hear him,
the boss-wren, out there in the summer dawn –

his bubbling sequences,
an octave higher than a blackbird's,
trickling silver seeds into my ears.

I'll get the tape-recorder.
But no, it's in another room,
and I've no blank tapes for it;

and anyway, I'm asleep.
Hard to wake up, after a sultry night
of restless dozing, even for the wren.

I've tracked his piccolo solo
in the light evenings, from hedge to apple tree
to elder, sprints of zippy flight in between.

I've looked him up: 'A rapid
succession of penetrating and jubilant
trills, very loud for so small a bird.'

I'll get the tape-recorder.
I'll find an old cassette to record over.
I'm getting up to fetch it now –

but no, I'm still asleep;
it was a dream, the getting up.
But the wren's no dream. It *is* a wren.


## Next Door

You could have called it the year of their persecution:
some villain robbed her window-boxes of half
her petunias and pansies. She wrote a notice:
'To the person who took my plants. I am disabled;
they cost me much labour to raise from seed.'
Next week, the rest went. Then his number-plates.
(Not the car itself. Who'd want the car? It stank.)
A gale blew in a pane of their front window –
crack: just like that. Why theirs? Why not, for example,
mine? Same gale; same row of elderly houses.

And through it all the cats multiplied fatly –
fatly but scruffily (his weak heart, her illness:
'They need grooming, I know, but they're fat as butter') –
and the fleas hopped, and the smell came through the walls.
How many cats? Two dozen? Forty? Fifty?
We could count the ones outside in the cages (twelve),
but inside? Always a different furry face
at a window; and the kittens – think of the kittens
pullulating like maggots over the chairs!
Someone reported them to the authorities.

Who could have done it? Surely not a neighbour!
'No, not a neighbour! Someone in the Fancy' –
she was certain. 'They've always envied my success.
The neighbours wouldn't...' A sunny afternoon.
I aimed my camera at them over the fence,
at their garden table, under the striped umbrella:
'Smile!' And they grinned: his gnome-hat, her witch-hair
in the sun – well out of earshot of the door-bell
and of the Environmental Health Inspector.
You could call it a bad year. But the next was worse.

# Heliopsis Scabra

This is the time of year when people die:
August, and these daisy-faced things
blare like small suns on their swaying hedge
of leaves, yellow as terror. Goodbye,

they shout to the summer, and goodbye
to Jim, whose turn it was this morning:
while in another hospital his wife
lies paralysed, with nothing to do but lie

wondering what's being kept from her, and cry –
she can still do that. August in hospital
sweats and is humid. In the garden
grey airs blow moist, but the mean sky

holds on to its water. The earth's coke-dry;
the yellow daisies goggle, but other plants
less greedily rooted are at risk.
The sky surges and sulks. It will let them die.


# House-martins

Mud in their beaks, the house-martins are happy...
That's anthropomorphism. Start again:

mud being plentiful because last night
it rained, after a month of drought,
the house-martins are able to build their nests.

They flitter under the eaves, white flashes
on their backs telling what they are:
house-martins. Not necessarily happy.

Below in the mock-Tudor cul-de-sac
two kids on skateboards and a smaller girl
with a tricycle are sketching their own circles –

being themselves, being children:
vaguely aware, perhaps, of the house-martins,
and another bird singing, and a scent of hedge.

Anthropomorphism tiptoes away:
of human children it's permissible
to say they're happy – if indeed they are.

It's no use asking them; they wouldn't know.
They may be bored, or in a sulk,
or worried (it doesn't show; and they look healthy).

Ask them in fifty years or so,
if they're still somewhere. Arrange to present them with
(assuming all these things can still be assembled)

a blackbird's song, the honeyed reek of privet,
and a flock of house-martins, wheeling and scrambling
about a group of fake-half-timbered semis.

Call it a Theme Park, if you like:
'Suburban childhood, late 1980s'
(or 70s, or 50s – it's hardly changed).

Ask them 'Were you happy in Shakespeare Close?'
and watch them gulp, sick with nostalgia for it.


## Wildlife


A wall of snuffling snouts in close-up,
ten coloured, two in black and white,
each in its frame; all magnified,
some more than others. Voles, are they?
Shrews? Water-rats? Whiskers waggling,
they peep from under twelve tree-roots
and vanish. Next, a dozen barn-owls,
pale masks, almost filling the dark screens.
Cut; and now two dozen hedgehogs
come trotting forward in headlong pairs:
they'll fall right out on the floor among the
cookers and vacuum-cleaners unless
the camera – just in time – draws back.
Here they come again, in their various
sizes, on their various grass:
olive, emerald, acid, bluish,

dun-tinged, or monochrome. The tones
are best, perhaps, on the 22-inch
ITT Squareline: more natural
than the Philips – unless you find them too
muted, in which case the Sony
might do. Now here are the owls again.

Meanwhile at the Conference Centre
three fire-engines have screamed up. Not,
for once, a student smoking in a bedroom:
this time a cloud of thunderflies
has chosen to swarm on the pearly-pink
just-warm globe of a smoke-detector.

## Turnip-heads

Here are the ploughed fields of Middle England;
and here are the scarecrows, flapping polythene arms
over what still, for the moment, looks like England:
bare trees, earth-colours, even a hedge or two.

The scarecrows' coats are fertiliser bags;
their heads (it's hard to see from the swift windows
of the Intercity) are probably 5-litre
containers for some chemical or other.

And what are the scarecrows guarding? Fields of rape?
Plenty of that in Middle England; also
pillage, and certain other medieval
institutions – some things haven't changed,

now that the men of straw are men of plastic.
They wave their rags in fitful semaphore,
in the March wind; our train blurs past them.
Whatever their message was, we seem to have missed it.

# The Batterer

What can I have done to earn
the Batterer striding here beside me,
checking up with his blue-china
sidelong eyes that I've not been bad –

not glanced across the street, forgetting
to concentrate on what he's saying;
not looked happy without permission,
or used the wrong form of his name?

How did he get here, out of the past,
with his bulging veins and stringy tendons,
fists clenched, jaw gritted,
about to burst with babble and rage?

Did I elect him? Did I fall
asleep and vote him in again?
Yes, that'll be what he is: a nightmare;
but someone else's now, not mine.


# Roles

Emily Brontë's cleaning the car:
water sloshes over her old trainers
as she scrubs frail blood-shapes from the windscreen
and swirls the hose-jet across the roof.
When it's done she'll go to the supermarket;
then, if she has to, face her desk.

I'm striding on the moor in my hard shoes,
a shawl over my worsted bodice,
the hem of my skirt scooping dew from the grass
as I pant up towards the breathless heights.
I'll sit on a rock I know and write a poem.
It may not come out as I intend.

# Happiness

Too jellied, viscous, floating a condition
to inspire more action than a sigh –
like being supported on warm porridge

gazing at this: may-blossom, bluebells, robin,
the tennis-players through the trees,
the trotting magpie (not good news, but handsome)

asking the tree-stump next to where I'm sitting
'Were you a rowan last time? No?
That's what the seedling wedged in your roots is planning.'


# Coupling

On the wall above the bedside lamp
a large crane-fly is jump-starting
a smaller crane-fly – or vice versa.
They do it tail to tail, like Volkswagens:
their engines must be in their rears.

It looks easy enough. Let's try it.


# The Greenhouse Effect

As if the week had begun anew –
and certainly something has:
this fizzing light on the harbour, these
radiant bars and beams and planes
slashed through flaps and swags of sunny vapour.
Aerial water, submarine light:
Wellington's gone Wordsworthian again.
He'd have admired it –
admired but not approved, if he'd heard
about fossil fuels, and aerosols,
and what we've done to the ozone layer,
or read in last night's *Evening Post*

that 'November ended the warmest spring
since meteorological records began'.
Not that it wasn't wet:
moisture's a part of it.

As for this morning (Friday),
men in shorts raking the beach
have constructed little cairns of evidence:
driftwood, paper, plastic cups.
A seagull's gutting a bin.
The rain was more recent than I thought:
I'm sitting on a wet bench.
Just for now, I can live with it.


## The Last Moa


Somewhere in the bush, the last moa
is not still lingering in some hidden valley.
She is not stretching her swanlike neck
(but longer, more massive than any swan's)
for a high cluster of miro berries,
or grubbing up fern roots with her beak.

Alice McKenzie didn't see her
among the sandhills at Martin's Bay
in 1880 – a large blue bird
as tall as herself, which turned and chased her.
Moas were taller than seven-year-old
pioneer children; moas weren't blue.

Twenty or thirty distinct species –
all of them, even the small bush moa,
taller than Alice – and none of their bones
carbon-dated to less than five centuries.
The sad, affronted mummified head
in the museum is as old as a Pharoah.

Not the last moa, that; but neither
was Alice's harshly grunting pursuer.
Possibly Alice met a takahe,
the extinct bird that rose from extinction
in 1948, near Te Anau.
No late reprieve, though, for the moa.

Her thigh-bones, longer than a giraffe's,
are lying steeped in a swamp, or smashed
in a midden, with her unstrung vertebrae.
Our predecessors hunted and ate her,
gobbled her up: as we'd have done
in their place; as we're gobbling the world.


## Creosote

What is it, what is it? Quick: that whiff,
that black smell – black that's really brown,
sharp that's really oily and yet rough,

a tang of splinters burning the tongue,
almost as drunkening as hot tar
or cowshit, a wonderful ringing pong.

It's fence-posts, timber yards, the woodshed;
it bundles you into the Baby Austin
and rushes you back to early childhood.

It's Uncle's farm; it's the outside dunny;
it's flies and heat; or it's boats and rope
and the salt-cracked slipway down from the jetty.

It's brushes oozing with sloshy stain;
it's a tin at the back of the shed: open it,
snort it! You can't: the lid's stuck on.


## Central Time

'The time is nearly one o'clock,
or half past twelve in Adelaide' –
where the accents aren't quite so... Australian
as in the other states, the ones
that were settled (not their fault, of course)
by convicts. We had Systematic
Colonisation, and Colonel Light,
and the City of Adelaide Plan. We have the Park Lands.

It's time for the news at 1.30 –
one o'clock Central Time in Adelaide.

It's early days in Hobart Town,
and Maggie May has been transported
(not such fun as it sounds, poor lass)
to toil upon Van Diemen's cruel shore.
It's 1830 or thereabouts
(1800 in Adelaide?
No, no, this is going too far –
as she might have said herself at the time).

The time is three o'clock, etc.
The time is passing.
You're tuned to ABC Radio.
We'll be bringing you that programme shortly.

It's five o'clock in Adelaide
and Maggie May has found her way
to a massage parlour in Gouger Street.
The Red Light Zone (as we don't call it)
extends from the West Park Lands to Light Square
(named for the Colonel, not the Zone).
The Colonel's in two minds about it;
his fine Eurasian face is troubled.

The Colonel's an anomaly.
There are plenty of those in Adelaide.
Meanwhile, back in Van Diemen's Land,
a butcher bird sings coloratura
in the courtyard of the Richmond Gaol
as tourists file through with their cameras,
wondering how to photograph
a Dark Cell for solitary
from the inside, with the door shut.
Look, they had them for women too!

It's half past eight in Adelaide
and 4 a.m. in Liverpool.
Maggie May wants to ring Lime Street.
You mean they don't have STD?
But I thought this was the New World.

They don't have GMT either;
or BST, as they call it now,
whenever now is.

207

It is now
half past ten in Adelaide,
and in the Park Lands a nasty man
is cutting up a teenage boy
and cramming him into a plastic bag.

In Gouger Street another man,
equally nasty but less wicked,
has taken his wife to a performance
of Wagner at the Opera Theatre
and is strolling with her to their car
past the massage parlour
where something like five hours ago
Maggie May gave him a hand-job.

The Colonel's brooding over his notebooks,
and lying under his stone, and standing
on his plinth on Montefiore Hill.

Maggie May is still on the phone,
arguing with the operator,
trying to get through to Lime Street.
It's the future she wants,
or the past back. Some of it.

You're listening to ABC FM:
12.30 Eastern Standard Time –
twelve midnight in Adelaide.
And now, to take us through the night,
Music to Keep the Days Apart.

## The Breakfast Program

May: autumn. In more or less recognisable
weather, more or less recognisable birds
are greeting the dawn. On 5CL the newsreader
has been allotted (after the lead story
on whether the Treasurer might or still might not
cancel the promised tax-cuts) two minutes
to tell us about whatever it is today –
chemical weapons, radioactive rain,
one of those messy bits of northern gloom
from the places where gloom's made (not here, not here!).

He tells us; then the baby-talking presenter
(curious how some Australian women
never get to sound older than fifteen)
contrives a soothing link: 'Grim news indeed,'
she ad-libs cosily. 'Much worse, of course,
if you live in Europe' – writing off a hemisphere.


# From the Demolition Zone


Come, literature, and salve our wounds:
bring dressings, antibiotics, morphine;

bring syringes, oxygen, plasma.
(Saline solution we have already.)

We're injured, but we mustn't say so;
it hurts, but we mustn't tell you where.

Clear-eyed literature, diagnostician,
be our nurse and our paramedic.

Hold your stethoscope to our hearts
and tell us what you hear us murmuring.

Scan us; but do it quietly, like
the quiet seep of our secret bleeding.

When we lie awake in the night
cold and shaking, clenching our teeth,

be the steady hand on our pulse,
the skilful presence checking our symptoms.

You know what we're afraid of saying
in case they hear us. Say it for us.

# On the Way to the Castle

It would be rude to look out of the car windows
at the colourful peasants authentically pursuing
their traditional activities in the timeless landscape
while the editor is talking to us.
He is telling us about the new initiatives
his magazine has adopted as a result
of the Leader's inspiring speech at the last Party Congress.
He is speaking very slowly (as does the Leader,
whom we have seen on our hotel television),
and my eyes are politely fixed on his little moustache:
as long as it keeps moving they will have to stay there;
but when he pauses for the interpreter's turn
my duty is remitted, and I can look out of the windows.
I am not ignoring the interpreter's translation
but she has become our friend: I do not feel compelled
by courtesy to keep my eyes on her lipstick.
What's more, the editor has been reciting his speech
at so measured a pace and with such clarity
that I can understand it in his own language;
and in any case, I have heard it before.
This on-off pattern of switching concentration
between the editor's moustache and the sights we are passing
gives me a patchy impression of the local agriculture.
Hordes of head-scarved and dark-capped figures
move through fields of this and that, carrying implements,
or bending and stretching, or loading things on to carts.
I missed most of a village, during the bit about the print-run,
but the translation granted me a roadful of quaint sheep.
Now the peasants are bent over what looks like bare earth
with occasional clusters of dry vegetation.
It is a potato field; they are grubbing for potatoes.
There are dozens of them – of peasants, that is:
the potatoes themselves are not actually visible.
As a spectacle, this is not notably picturesque,
but I should like to examine it for a little longer.
The sky has turned black; it is beginning to rain.
The editor has thought of something else he wishes to tell us
about the magazine's history.
Once again, eyes back to his official moustache
(under which his unofficial mouth looks vulnerable).
The editor is a kind man.
He is taking us on an interesting excursion,
in an expensive taxi, during his busy working day.

It has all been carefully planned for our pleasure.
Quite possibly he wants to shield us from the fact
that this rain is weeks or months too late;
that the harvest is variously scorched, parched and withered;
that the potatoes for which the peasants are fossicking
have the size and the consistency of bullets.


## Romania


Suddenly it's gone public; it rushed out
into the light like a train out of a tunnel.
People I've met are faces in the government,
shouting on television, looking older.

The country sizzles with freedom. The air-waves
tingle. The telephone lines are all jammed.
I can't get through to my friends. Are they safe? They're safe,
but I need to hear it from them. Instead

I'll play the secret tape I made in the orchard
two years ago, at Ciorogîla.
We're talking in two languages, mine and theirs,
laughing, interrupting each other;

the geese in the peasants' yard next door
are barking like dogs; the children are squawking,
chasing each other, picking fruit;
the little boy brings me a flower and a carrot.

We're drinking must – blood-pink, frothy –
and a drop of unofficial *ţuica*:
'What do the peasants drink in your country? –
Oh, I forgot, you don't have peasants.'

It's dusk. The crickets have started up:
Zing-zing, zing-zing, like telephones
over the static. Did it really happen?
Is it possible? 'Da, da!' say the geese.

*December 1989*

*Causes*

## The Farm
*(in memory of Fiona Lodge)*

Fiona's parents need her today –
they're old; one's ill, and slipping away –
but Fiona won't be by the bed:
                         she's dead.
She went for a working holiday
years ago, on a farm that lay
just down the coast from St Bee's Head
in Cumbria, next to – need I say?
                         A name to dread.
She was always very fond of the farm
with its rough, authentic rural charm,
and the fields she tramped, and the lambs she fed
                         with youthful pride.
Her family saw no cause for alarm –
how could it do her any harm
working there in the countryside?
It would help to build her up, they said.
But it secretly broke her down instead,
                         until she died.
There was a leak, if you recall,
at Windscale in the fifties. No?
Well, it was thirty years ago;
                         but these things are slow.
And no matter what the authorities said
about there being no risk at all
from the installations at Calder Hall,
buckets of radiation spread,
                         and people are dead.
That farm became a hazardous place –
though to look at it you wouldn't know;
but cancers can take years to grow
(or leukaemia, in Fiona's case),
and as often as not they win the race,
                         however slow.
Before long most of us will know
people who've died in a similar way.
We're not aware of it today,
                         and nor are they,

but another twenty years or so
will sort out who are the ones to go.
We'll be able to mark them on a chart,
a retrospective map to show
where the source of their destruction lay.
                    That's the easy part.
But where's the next lot going to start?
At Windscale, Hinkley Point, Dounreay,
Dungeness, Sizewell, Druridge Bay?
                    Who can say?


## Aluminium


*Ting-ting!* 'What's in your pocket, sir?'
*Ping!* Metal. Not coins or keys:
Sterotabs for the foreign water,
armour against one kind of disease.

'Aluminium: that's what they are –
they set the machine off.' That's it, then:
out of the frying-pan into the fire;
here's awful Alzheimer's looming again.

There wasn't much point in throwing away
your aluminium pots and kettle
if whenever you go on holiday
your drinking water's full of that metal.

Which will you swallow: bacteria soup,
or a clanking cocktail of sinister granules
that'll rust your mental circuitry up
and knot your brain-cells into tangles?

Don't bother to choose. You can't abjure it,
the use of this stuff to "purify".
At home the Water Board's fallen for it:
don't be surprised to see a ring of sky,

grey and canny as a metal detector,
to hear, amidst an aerial hum,
tintinnabulations over the reservoir
warning you of dementia to come.

# A Hymn to Friendship

Somehow we manage it: to like our friends,
to tolerate not only their little ways
but their huge neuroses, their monumental oddness:
'Oh well,' we smile, 'it's one of his funny days.'

Families, of course, are traditionally awful:
embarrassing parents, ghastly brothers, mad aunts
provide a useful training-ground to prepare us
for the pseudo-relations we acquire by chance.

Why them, though? Why not the woman in the library
(grey hair, big mouth) who reminds us so of J?
Or the one on Budgen's delicatessen counter
(shy smile, big nose) who strongly resembles K?

– Just as the stout, untidy gent on the train
reading the *Mail on Sunday* through pebble specs
could, with somewhat sparser hair and a change
of reading-matter, be our good friend X.

True, he isn't; they aren't; but why does it matter?
Wouldn't they do as well as the friends we made
in the casual past, by being at school with them,
or living nextdoor, or learning the same trade?

Well, no, they wouldn't. Imagine sharing a tent
with one of these look-alikes, and finding she snored:
no go. Or listening for days on end while she dithered
about her appalling marriage: we'd be bored.

Do we feel at all inclined to lend them money?
Or travel across a continent to stay
for a weekend with them? Or see them through an abortion,
a divorce, a gruelling court-case? No way.

Let one of these impostors desert his wife
for a twenty-year-old, then rave all night about
her sensitivity and her gleaming thighs,
while guzzling all our whisky: we'd boot him out.

And as for us, could we ring them up at midnight
when our man walked out on us, or our roof fell in?
Would they offer to pay our fare across the Atlantic
to visit them? The chances are pretty thin.

Would they forgive our not admiring their novel,
or saying we couldn't really take to their child,
or confessing that years ago we went to bed
with their husband? No, they wouldn't: they'd go wild.

Some things kindly strangers will put up with,
but we need to know exactly what they are:
it's OK to break a glass, if we replace it,
but we mustn't let our kids be sick in their car.

Safer to stick with people who remember
how we ourselves, when we and they were nineteen,
threw up towards the end of a student party
on ethyl alcohol punch and methedrine.

In some ways we've improved since then. In others
(we glance at the heavy jowls and thinning hair,
hoping we're slightly better preserved than they are)
at least it's a deterioration we share.

It can't be true to say that we chose our friends,
or surely we'd have gone for a different lot,
while they, confronted with us, might well have decided
that since it was up to them they'd rather not.

But something keeps us hooked, now we're together,
a link we're not so daft as to disparage –
nearly as strong as blood-relationship
and far more permanent, thank God, than marriage.

## Smokers for Celibacy

Some of us are a little tired of hearing that cigarettes kill.
We'd like to warn you about another way of making yourself ill:

we suggest that in view of AIDS, herpes, chlamydia, cystitis and NSU,
not to mention genital warts and cervical cancer and the proven connection
     between the two,

if you want to avoid turning into physical wrecks
what you should give up is not smoking but sex.

We're sorry if you're upset,
but think of the grisly things you might otherwise get.

We can't see much point in avoiding emphysema at sixty-five
if that's an age at which you have conspicuously failed to arrive;

and as for cancer, it is a depressing fact
that at least for women this disease is more likely to occur in the reproductive
        tract.

We could name friends of ours who died that way, if you insist,
but we feel sure you can each provide your own list.

You'll notice we didn't mention syphilis and gonorrhoea;
well, we have now, so don't get the idea

that just because of antibiotics quaint old clap and pox
are not still being generously spread around by men's cocks.

Some of us aren't too keen on the thought of micro-organisms travelling up
        into our brain
and giving us General Paralysis of the Insane.

We're opting out of one-night stands;
we'd rather have a cigarette in our hands.

If it's a choice between two objects of cylindrical shape
we go for the one that is seldom if ever guilty of rape.

Cigarettes just lie there quietly in their packs
waiting until you call on one of them to help you relax.

They aren't moody; they don't go in for sexual harassment and threats,
or worry about their performance as compared with that of other cigarettes,

nor do they keep you awake all night telling you the story of their life,
beginning with their mother and going on until morning about their first wife.

Above all, the residues they leave in your system are thoroughly sterilised and
        clean,
which is more than can be said for the products of the human machine.

Altogether, we've come to the conclusion that sex is a drag.
Just give us a fag.

# Mrs Fraser's Frenzy
*Songs for Music*

### 1

My name is Eliza Fraser.
I belong to some savages.
My job is to feed the baby
they have hung on my shoulder.

Its mother is lying sick
with no milk in her breasts,
and my own baby died:
it was born after the shipwreck.

It was born under water
in the ship's leaky longboat.
Three days I helped to bail,
then gave birth in the scuppers.

My poor James, the captain,
was crippled with thirst and sickness.
The men were all useless,
and no woman to call on.

I believe the First Mate,
Mr Brown, treated me kindly;
he consigned my dead infant
to its watery fate.

But now I have been given
a black child to suckle.
I have been made a wet-nurse,
a slave to savage women.

They taunt me and beat me.
They make me grub for lily-roots
and climb trees for honey.
They poke burning sticks at me.

They have rubbed me all over
with charcoal and lizard-grease
to protect me from sunburn.
It is my only cover.

I am as black as they are
and almost as naked,
with stringy vines for a loincloth
and feathers stuck in my hair.

They are trying to change me
into one of themselves.
My name is Eliza Fraser.
I pray God to save me.

Their men took my husband –
they dragged him into the forest –
but I still have my wedding-ring
concealed in my waistband.

My name is Eliza Fraser.
My home is in Stromness.
I have left my three children
in the care of the minister.

I am a strong woman.
My language is English.
My name is Eliza Fraser
and my age thirty-seven.


2

The ghosts came from the sea, the white ghosts.
One of them was a she-ghost, a white woman.
We took her to the camp, the white she-ghost.
She was white all over, white like the ancestors,
white like the bodies of dead people
when you scorch them in the fire and strip off the skin.
She was a ghost, but we don't know whose.
We asked her 'Whose ghost are you?
Which ancestor has come back to us?'
She wouldn't say. She had forgotten our language.
She talked in a babble like the babble of birds,
that ghost from the sea, that white she-ghost.
She was covered with woven skins, but we stripped her;
she had hairs on her body, but we plucked them out;
we tried to make her look like a person.
She was stupid, though. She wouldn't learn.
We talked to her and she didn't listen.
We told her to go out and collect food, to dig for roots.
We told her to climb trees, to look for honey.

She couldn't, not even when we beat her.
She seems to have forgotten everything,
that ghost from the sea, that white woman.
We send her out for food every day
and she brings back a few bits, not enough for a child.
We have to throw her scraps, or she would starve.
All she is fit for is to suckle a baby,
that ancestor woman, that white ghost.
We have put her among the children until she learns.


3

I am a poor widow.
I do not own a farthing –
bereft in a shipwreck
of all but my wedding-ring.

　　You are a liar, Mrs Fraser.
　　You own two trunks of finery
　　and £400 subscribed
　　by the citizens of Sydney.

I am a poor widow.
My fatherless children
are alone up in Orkney
while I beg for money.

The Lord Mayor of Liverpool,
the Lord Mayor of London,
the Colonial Secretary:
they will none of them help me.

　　You are a liar, Mrs Fraser.
　　You are not even Mrs Fraser.
　　You have another husband now –
　　you married Captain Greene in Sydney.

I am a poor widow,
the victim of cannibals.
They killed my dear husband
on the shores of New Holland.

They skinned him and baked him;
they cut up his body
and gorged on his flesh
in their villainous gluttony.

Their hair is bright blue,
those abominable monsters;
it grows in blue tufts
on the tips of their shoulders...

You are a liar, Mrs Fraser.
Your sad ordeals have quite unhinged you.
You were a decent woman once,
prickly with virtue. What has changed you?
Tell us the truth, the truth, the truth!
What really happened that deranged you?


4

Not easy to love Mrs Fraser.
Captain Fraser managed it, in his time –
hobbling on her arm, clutching his ulcer,
falling back to relieve his griping bowels;
and hauling timber, a slave to black masters:
'Eliza, wilt thou help me with this tree? –
Because thou art now stronger than me.'
But they speared him, and she fainted, just that once.

Her children had to love her from a distance –
from Orkney to the far Antipodes,
or wherever she'd sailed off to with their father,
cosseting him with jellies for his gut:
'I have received a letter from dear Mamma.
I am looking for her daily at Stromness.'
Daily they had no sight of Mrs Fraser –
who had secretly turned into Mrs Greene.

And Captain Greene? Did he contrive to love her?
He never saw her as her rescuers did:
'Perfectly black, and crippled from her sufferings,
a mere skeleton, legs a mass of sores.'
He saw a widow, famous, with some money.
He saw the chance of more. He saw, perhaps,
a strangeness in her, gone beyond the strangeness
of anything he'd met on the seven seas.

5

I am not mad. I sit in my booth
on show for sixpence: 'Only survivor'
(which is a lie) 'of the *Stirling Castle*
wrecked off New Holland' (which is the truth),

embroidering facts. There is no need
to exaggerate (but I do), to sit
showing my scars to gawping London.
I do it for money. This is not greed:

I am not greedy. I am not mad.
I have a husband. I am cared for.
But I wake in the nights howling, naked,
alone, and starving. All that I had

I lost once – all the silken stuff
of civilisation: clothes, possessions,
decency, liberty, my name;
and now I can never get enough

to replace it. There can never be
enough of anything in the world,
money or goods, to keep me warm
and fed and clothed and safe and free.

# Meeting the Comet

**1**

She'll never be able to play the piano –
well, not properly. She'll never be able
to play the recorder, even, at school,
when she goes: it has so many little holes...

We'll have her taught the violin.
Lucky her left hand's the one with four
fingers, one for each string. A thumb
and a fleshy fork are enough to hold a bow.


**2**

Before the calculator – the electronic one –
there were beads to count on; there was the abacus
to tell a tally or compute a score;
or there were your fingers, if you had enough.

The base was decimal: there had to be
a total of ten digits, in two sets –
a bunch of five, another bunch of five.
If they didn't match, your computations went haywire.


**3**

On the left hand, four      and a thumb.
On the right, a thumb       and just two.
Proper fingers, true,       fitted out
in the standard way;        but not four.

Baby-plump, the wrist       on the left.
On the right, the arm       narrows down
to a slender stem           and a palm
like a little tube          of soft bones.

222

4

Leafy lanes and *rus in urbe* were the thing
for a sheltered childhood (not that it was for long,
but parents try): the elm trees lingering
behind the coach factory; the tense monotonous song

of collared doves; the acres of bare floor
for learning to gallop on in the first size
of Start-Rite shoes; the peacock glass in the front door;
and the swift refocusing lurch of the new baby-sitter's eyes.


5

The Duke of Edinburgh stance: how cute
in a five-year-old! She doesn't do it much
when you're behind her; then it's hands in armpits
or pockets. School, of course, would like to teach

that well-adjusted children don't need pockets
except for their normal purposes, to hold
hankies or bus-tickets. She'll not quite learn
what she's not quite specifically taught.


6

Perhaps I don't exist. Perhaps
I didn't exist till I thought that;
then God invented me and made me
the age I am now (nearly eight);

perhaps I was someone else before,
and he suddenly swapped us round, and said
'You can be the girl with two fingers
and she can be you for a change, instead.'


7

'Give us your hand – it's a bit muddy here,
you'll slip.' But he's on her wrong side: her right's
wrong. She tries to circumnavigate him
('Watch it!' he says), to offer him her left –

and slips. It comes out. 'There!' she says. 'You see!'
'Is that all? Fucking hell,' he says, 'that's nothing;
don't worry about it, love. My Auntie May
lost a whole arm in a crash. Is it hereditary?'


8

'Some tiny bud that should have split into four
didn't, we don't know why' was all they could offer.
Research, as usual, lags. But suddenly, this:
'A long-term study has found a positive link

between birth defects and exposure to pesticides
in the first twelve weeks of pregnancy... the baby's
neural crest... mothers who had been present when
aerosol insecticides...' Now they tell us.


TRAVELLING

9 *So Far*

She has not got multiple sclerosis.
She has not got motorneuron disease,
or muscular dystrophy, or Down's Syndrome,
or a cleft palate, or a hole in the heart.

Her sight and hearing seem to be sound.
She has not been damaged by malnutrition,
or tuberculosis, or diabetes.
She has not got (probably not got) cancer.


10 *Passport*

Date of birth and all that stuff: straightforward;
likewise, now that she's stopped growing, height.
But ah, 'Distinguishing marks': how can she smuggle
so glaring a distinction out of sight?

The Passport Office proves, in one of its human
incarnations, capable of tact:
a form of words emerges that fades down
her rare statistic to a lustreless fact.

## 11  *Stars*

She's seeing stars – Orion steady on her left
like a lit-up kite (she has a window-seat),
and her whole small frame of sky strung out
with Christmas-tree lights. But what's all that

behind them? Spilt sugar? Spangled faults
in the plane's window? A dust of glittering points
like the sparkle-stuff her mother wouldn't let her
wear on her eyes to the third-form party.


## 12  *Halfway*

Does less mean more? She's felt more nearly naked
in duffel-coat and boots and scarf
with nothing showing but a face and her bare
fingers (except, of course, for the times

in fur gloves – mittens – look, no hands!)
than here on a beach in a bikini:
flesh all over. Look at my legs, my
back, my front. Shall I take off my top?


## 13  *At the Airport*

Shoulders like horses' bums; an upper arm
dressed in a wobbling watermelon of flesh
and a frilly muu-muu sleeve; red puckered necks
above the bougainvillaea and sunsets

and straining buttons of Hawaiian shirts;
bellies, bald heads, a wilting grey moustache
beneath a hat proclaiming 'One Old Poop'.
The tour guide rounds them up: his travelling freak-show.


## 14  *Comet*

'There will be twenty telescopes in the crater
of Mount Albert.' White-coated figures man them,
marshalling queues in darkness: not the Klan
but the Lions raising funds for charity.

$2 a look. No lights – not even torches;
no smoking (bad for the optics); no moon
above the tree-fringed walls of this grassy dip.
Nothing up there but stars. And it, of course.


15  *Halley Party*

A glow-worm in a Marmite jar
like the one her mother brought her once:
'I dreamt you woke me in the night and showed me
a glow-worm in a Marmite jar.'

So these wee kids in dressing-gowns
will remember being woken up
for honey sandwiches and cocoa
and a little light in a ring of glass.


16  *Orbit*

'It's not like anything else, with its stumpy tail:
just a fuzz, really, until you get up close –
but of course you can't. With binoculars, I meant,
or a telescope. Actually the tail's fading.'

Higher than Scorpius now, higher than the Pointers,
high as the mid-heaven, she's tracked it nightly,
changing. 'I'm not the only one, but I'm once
in a lifetime.' As for close, that's something else.


AFTER

17

Landing at Gatwick on a grey Sunday when
the baggage handlers seem to be on strike as
they were at the airport before last (but no,
it's merely Britain being its old self) she's

her old self – a self consisting also of
more hand-luggage than she'd thought she was allowed
plus her at last reclaimed suitcase: all of which,
however she may dispose them, hurt her hand.

18

Rise above it! Swallow a chemical:
chuck down whisky, Valium, speed,
Mogadon, caffeine; bomb it or drown it.
But wait! If chemicals did the deed

pandering to their ways compounds
the offence. Resist: you know they lead
to trouble. Find another obsession.
Face a healthier form of need.


19

Saving the world is the only valid cause.
Now that she knows it's round it seems smaller,
more vulnerable (as well as bigger, looser,
a baggy bundle of dangerous contradictions).

There's room for such concerns in student life,
if you stretch it. So: Link hands around the world
for peace! Thumbs down to Star Wars! Hands off
the environment! Two fingers to the Bomb!


20

'Of course you'd have a natural sympathy...
I always thought it was quite sweet, your little hand,
when we were kids; but we don't want other kids
walking around the world with worse things...

I'm not upsetting you, am I?' No, she's not,
this warm voice from the past, this candid face.
'Right. See you tomorrow. The coach leaves at 8.
Oh, and we've got a wonderful furious banner.'


21

The fountain in her heart informs her
she needn't try to sleep tonight –
rush, gush: the sleep-extinguisher
frothing in her chest like a dishwasher.

She sits at the window with a blanket
to track the turning stars. A comet
might add some point. The moon ignores her;
but dawn may come. She'd settle for that.


## 22

There was a young woman who fell
for someone she knew rather well –
a friend from her school: confirming the rule
that with these things you never can tell.

The person she'd thought a fixed star –
stuck on rails like a tram, not a car –
shot off into orbit and seemed a new planet,
and a dazzler, the finest by far.


## 23

She wants to see what it looks like on
a breast. She puts it on a breast –
not the one she has in mind
but her own: at least it's a rehearsal.

Three weeks later, the first night:
a nipple, darker than hers, framed
in a silky, jointed bifurcation.
There is also dialogue. And applause.


## 24

And she never did learn to play the violin.
So it will have to be *Musica Mundana*,
'the harmony of the spheres' (coming across a map
of the southern skies cut out of some Auckland paper)

or the other kind: what was it? *Instrumentalis*
and – ah, yes – *Humana*. (Listen: Canopus, Crux,
Carina, Libra, Vela choiring together. She
has glided right off the edge of the star-chart.)

# LOOKING BACK

(1997)

# I

## Where They Lived

That's where they lived in the 1890s.
They don't know that we know,
or that we're standing here, in possession
of some really quite intimate information
about the causes of their deaths,
photographing each other in a brisk wind
outside their terrace house, both smiling
(not callously, we could assure them),
our hair streaming across our faces
and the green plastic Marks and Spencer's bag
in which I wrapped my camera against showers
ballooning out like a wind-sock
from my wrist, showing the direction
of something that's blowing down our century.


## Framed
*(Sam Adcock, 1876-1956, & Eva Eggington, 1875-1970)*

What shall we do with Grandpa, in his silver
frame? And why is he in it, may we ask?
Why not Grandma, still shyly veiled in her
tissue paper and photographer's cardboard?

Of course, there's his moustache: we can't miss that;
nor would he wish us to. It must have taken
hours and all his barbering skills to wax
and twirl the ends into these solemn curlicues.

We can't keep that in a drawer – or he couldn't.
But Grandma, now, in her black, nervously smiling,
one hand barely poised on the same ridiculous
Empire chairback: what a stunner she was!

Why did he not frame her? After all, her looks
are what he married her for. He fell in love
with her portrait (not this one) in a photographer's
window, and hunted down the woman herself.

234

She was a dressmaker's cutter (cool hands);
he was an extrovert – a talker, mixer
(the Lodge, the Church, the Mechanics' Institute,
the Temperance Movement). And it all came true:

seven years of engagement, fifty more
together. You can almost map their marriage,
decade by decade, through the evolution,
flourishing and decline of his moustache.

At twenty, not a whisker; at thirty or so,
this elaborate facial construct. In Manchester
it throve; then what did he do but export it
to droop and sag in the bush at Te Raua Moa,

on his dairy farm (how those cattle depressed him –
was New Zealand not such a bright idea after all?).
But it perked up for his passport in the 30s,
with a devilish Vandyke beard, for their last trip Home.

Not a handsome man, he must have decided
to take a bit of trouble and pass for one;
while Grandma, with the eyes and the bone structure
and that tilt of the head, decided to be plain.

She took to bobbed hair and wire-framed glasses,
and went grey early. He never did (unless
there was some preparation he knew about?)
Here they are in a 50s Polyfoto –

she with her shy smile, he with a muted version
of the moustache, wearing his cameo tie-pin
and a jubilant grin, as if he'd just slammed down
the winning trick in his favourite game of 'Sorry!'

# The Russian War

Great-great-great-uncle Francis Eggington
came back from the Russian War
(it was the kind of war you came back from,
if you were lucky: bad, but over).

235

He didn't come to the front door –
the lice and filth were falling off him –
he slipped along the alley to the yard.
'Who's that out at the pump?' they said
'– a tall tramp stripping his rags off!'
The soap was where it usually was.
He scrubbed and splashed and scrubbed,
and combed his beard over the hole in his throat.
'Give me some clothes,' he said. 'I'm back.'
'God save us, Frank, it's you!' they said.
'What happened? Were you at Scutari?
And what's that hole inside your beard?'
'Tea first,' he said. 'I'll tell you later.
And Willie's children will tell their grandchildren;
I'll be a thing called oral history.'


## 227 Peel Green Road


Failing their flesh and bones we have the gatepost.
Failing the bride in her ostrich-feathered hat,
the groom bracing his shoulders for the camera,
we have the garden wall, the path, and the gatepost:

not the original gatepost, but positioned
in exactly the same relation to the house –
just as the windows have been modernised
but we can see their dimensions are the same

as the ones behind the handsome brothers' heads
under their wedding bowlers. The gatepost
stands to the left, where nine-year-old Nellie
ought to be standing, in her home-made dress,

her boots and stockings and white hair-ribbon,
leaning her wistful head against Marion –
her next-best sister, who will have to do
now that Eva's married and going away.

Father and Mother, corpulent on chairs,
young Harry wincing in his Fauntleroy collar,
James in his first hard hat, a size too large,
have faded away from bricks and wood and metal.

Failing the sight of Mary, flowered and frilled,
the married sister, simpering on the arm
of Abraham with his curled moustache (the swine:
he'll leave her, of course) we may inspect the drainpipe:

not the authentic late-Victorian drainpipe
but just where that one was, convincing proof
(together with the gatepost and the windows)
that this is it, all right: the very house –

unless it's not; unless that was a stand-in,
one the photographer preferred that day
and lined them up in front of, because the sun
was shining on it; as it isn't now.


## Nellie

*(i.m. Nellie Eggington, 1894-1913)*

Just because it was so long ago
doesn't mean it ceases to be sad.
Nellie on the sea-front at Torquay
watching the fishing-boats ('Dear Sis and Bro,
I am feeling very much better') had
six months left to die of her TB.

She and Marion caught it at the mill
from a girl who coughed and coughed across her loom.
Their father caught it; he and Marion died;
the others quaked and murmured; James fell ill.
So here was Nellie, with her rented room,
carefully walking down to watch the tide.

When she'd first been diagnosed, she'd said
'Please, could Eva nurse me, later on,
when it's time, that is... if I get worse?'
Eva swallowed hard and shook her head
(and grieved for fifty years): she had her son
to consider. So their mother went as nurse.

Nellie took her parrot to Torquay –
her pet (as she herself had been a pet,
Eva's and her father's); she could teach
words to it in the evenings after tea,
talk to it when the weather was too wet
or she too frail for sitting on the beach.

Back in Manchester they had to wait,
looking out for letters every day,
or postcards for 'Dear Sis'. The winter passed.
Eva and Sam made plans to emigrate.
(Not yet, though. Later.) April came, and May –
bringing something from Torquay at last:

news. It was Tom's Alice who glanced out,
and called to Eva; Eva called to Sam:
'Look! Here's Mother walking up the road
with Nellie's parrot in its cage.' No doubt
now of what had happened. On she came,
steadily carrying her sharp-clawed load.


## Mary Derry


The first spring of the new century
and there I was, fallen pregnant!

Scarcely out of winter, even –
scarcely 1800 at all –

with not a bud on the trees yet
when the new thing budded in me.

They said I ought to have known better:
after all, I was over thirty.

William was younger; and men, of course…
but he came round fair in the end.

We couldn't sit the banns through,
giggled at for three Sundays –

not in Lichfield. He got a licence
and wedded me the next morning

in Armitage. July, it was
by then, and my loose gown bulging.

The babe was christened in Lichfield, though.
You knew he died? The wages of sin.

*

So this is where we began again:
Liverpool. Can you hear the seagulls?

A screeching city: seagulls and wagons,
drawbridges, floodgates, lifting-gear,

and warehouses huge as cathedrals.
We lived down by the Duke's Dock,

one lodging after another.
The family grew as the city grew.

William sat on his high stool
inscribing figures in a ledger.

My care was the children, bless them.
I ferried most of them safely through

the perilous waters of infancy,
and saw them married. Then I died.

*

Well, of course you know that.
And you know what of: consumption,

a word you don't use; an unwilled
legacy to go haunting down

one line of my long posterity
to Frank's son, and his son's son,

and fan out in a shuddering shadow
over the fourth generation.

And what I have to ask is:
was it the city's fault, or mine?

You can't answer me. All you hear
is a faint mewing among the seagulls.

# Moses Lambert: The Facts

The young cordwainer (yes, that's right)
got married at the Old Church –
it's Manchester Cathedral now.
That was the cheapest place to go.

They married you in batches there –
a list of names, a buzz of responses,
and 'You're all married,' said the clerk.
'Pair up outside.' (Like shoes, thought Moses.)

After the ceremony, though,
he and Maria waited on.
They had an extra thing to do:
their daughter needed christening.

The baby's age is not recorded.
The bride was over twenty-one –
full age. The bridegroom (never mind
what he might have said) was seventeen.

The young Queen was on the throne;
they'd have to be Victorians now.
Meanwhile, two more facts: they were
from Leeds. One of them had red hair.

# Samuel Joynson

He looked for it in the streets first,
and the sooty back alleys. It wasn't there.

He looked for it in the beer-house;
it dodged away as soon as he glimpsed it.

It certainly wasn't there at work,
raining down with the sawdust on to
his broad-brimmed hat as he stood sweating
in the pit under the snorting blade.

He looked all over the house for it –
the kitchen the scullery the parlour
the bedroom he shared with two of his brothers –
and shrugged. Of course it wasn't there.

So he tied a noose around where it should have been,
and slipped his head into it, for one last look.


## Amelia

It went like this: I married at 22,
in 1870. My daughter was born
the following year – Laura, we called her.
(No reason for the name – we just liked it.)
In '72 my brother hanged himself.
Laura died exactly a year later,
when I was pregnant with her brother Thomas
(named for my dead father). In '74
three things happened: my baby Thomas died,
then my sister; then I gave birth to John,
my first child to survive. He was a hunchback.
(I don't suppose you care for that expression;
well, call it what you like.) He lived to 20,
making the best of things, my poor brave lad.

After him, I got the knack of producing
healthy children. Or perhaps it was the gin.
Yes, I took to the bottle. Wouldn't you?
By the time it killed me I'd five living –
a little Band of Hope, a bright household
of teetotallers, my husband at their head.
I died of a stroke, officially; 'of drink'
wasn't spoken aloud for forty years.
These youngsters have my portrait proudly framed –
an old thing in a shawl, with a huge nose.
They also have a photograph – a maiden
with frightened eyes and a nose as trim as theirs.
Both are labelled 'Amelia'. Which one
was I? I couldn't have been both, they're sure.

# Barber

They set the boy to hairdressing –
you didn't need to be strong, or have
a straight back like other people.

It was the scissors he liked – their glitter
and snicker-snack; the arts, too,
of elegant shaping. Oh, and the razors.

He served his time, and qualified young;
it's on his death certificate:
'Hairdresser (Master). Age 20.'

In the next column, 'Spinal disease,
15 months. Abscess, 12 months.'
That sounds like cancer. It felt like blades

burning, slicing – a whole year
to play the Little Mermaid, walking
on knife-edges, with hand-glass and comb.


# Flames

Which redhead did I get my temper from?
I've made a short ancestral list
by hair-colour and moods. But, more to the point,
what are the odds on Alzheimer's?

Which ones went funny in their seventies?
Mary Ellen, perhaps, found in the coal-shed
hunting for her Ship Canal shares
after her fiery hair turned grey.

My hair's not red. I like flames, though.
When I get old and mad I'll play with them –
run the flimsy veils through my fingers
like orange plastic film, like parachute-silk.

My hands will scorch and wither, if I do.
I shall be safe and dead. It won't matter.
It's something to look forward to,
playing with fire. That, or deep water.

# Water

I met an ancestor in the lane.
She couldn't stop: she was carrying water.
It slopped and bounced from the stoup against her;
the side of her skirt was dark with the stain,
oozing chillingly down to her shoe.
I stepped aside as she trudged past me,
frowning with effort, shivering slightly
(an icy drop splashed my foot too).
The dress that brushed against me was rough.
She didn't smell the way I smell:
I tasted the grease and smoke in her hair.
Water that's carried is never enough.
She'd a long haul back from the well.

No, I didn't see her. But she was there.


# A Haunting

'Hoy!' A hand hooks me into a doorway:
'Here!' (No, that's not it: too many aitches;
they'd have been short of those, if I recall...)
'Oy, there!' (Never mind the aitches, it's his
breath now, gin and vinegar – I'm choking –
and fire on my neck; the hand grinding my shoulder.
I'm a head taller, nearly, but he's strong.)
'Look at me! I'm your ancestor.'

Eyes in a smudged face. Dark clothes. A hat...
'Look at me!' A stunted stump of a man.
Boots. No coat, although it's cold. A jacket
crumpled at the elbows. (I'm shivering.)
What kind of hair? If I can get
my hands to move, I'll push his hat off. There:
black, above a gleam of white skin (oh you poor
factory rat, you bastard you, my forebear!).

'Which one are you? Which ancestor?' Won't say.
Won't talk now. Stands there, shaking me now and then,
staring. Dark-haired – but then so were they all
in the photographs: brown hair, red hair, grey,

all dark for the cameras; and unsmiling.
This one's before photography,
still on the verge of things: a pre-Victorian,
pre-Temperance, pre-gentility; and angry.

He shows a snaggle of teeth (pre-dentistry);
means another thing now: 'Give us a kiss!'
No. No, I can't. 'Why not? You're family.'
That's not a family expression on his face.
'You're a woman, aren't you? One of ours?
A great-great-great-granddaughter?' He looks
younger than me, thirtyish. How do you talk
to a young man who's been dead a hundred years?

'Not unless you tell me who you are.'
'A part of you,' he cackles. 'Never mind
which part.' (Is it compulsory, I wonder,
to like one's ancestors? I couldn't stand
that laugh of his for long.) 'You were so set
on digging us up. You thought it was romantic,
like all that poetry they talk about
(not me – I can't read). Well, I'm what you dug.

So: what'll you give me for the favour, lass?
You wouldn't be on this earth if it weren't for me.'
That scorching gin-breath. 'Let me find my purse.'
We stagger together, a step or two, and I'm free.
His hat's on the cobbles. I rattle it full of money.
Not sovereigns, no: pound coins, worth less than a kiss –
base metal to him, proleptic wealth, no use
for more than a century to come. I'm sorry.


## The Wars


When they were having the Gulf War
I went to the 18th century.
I could see no glory in this life.

Awake half the night with the World Service,
then off on an early train for news –
secrets, discoveries, public knowledge

lurking on microfilm or parchment:
'I bequeath to my said daughter Mary Adcock
my Bedd and Bedding my oak Clothes Chest and Drawers

my Dressing Table and Looking Glass my Arm chair
my Clock standing in my said Dwelling house,
And one half part or share of all my Pewter.'

When it was over and not over,
and they offered us the Recession instead,
I went back further, pursuing the St Johns,

the Hampdens, the Wentworths to their deathbeds:
'Item I give to my wives sonne...'
(Ah, so she *had* been married before!)

'...Mr Edward Russell fiftie pounds,
and to John his brother ten pounds by the yeare
to be paid him soe long as he followes the warrs...'


## Sub Sepibus

*'Many of this parish in the years ensuing were marryed clandestinely,*
*i.e.* sub sepibus, *and were excommunicated for their labour.'*

Note after entries for 1667 in Parish Register for Syston, Leicestershire


Under a hedge was good enough for us,
my Tommy Toon and me –
under the blackthorn, under the may,
under the stars at the end of the day,
under his cloak I lay,
under the shining changes of the moon;
under Tom Toon.

No banns or prayer-book for the likes of us,
my Tommy Toon and me.
Tom worked hard at his frame all day
but summer nights he'd come out to play,
in the hedge or the hay,
and ply his shuttle to a different tune –
my merry Tom Toon.

The vicar excommunicated us,
my Tommy Toon and me.
We weren't the only ones to stray –
there are plenty who lay down where we lay
and have babes on the way.
I'll see my tickling bellyful quite soon:
another Tom Toon.


## Anne Welby
*(died 9 May 1770, Beeby, Leicestershire)*


For her gravestone to have been moved is OK.
I know she isn't here, under the nettles;
but what did I want to do, after all –
burrow into the earth and stroke her skull?

Would that help me to see her? Would she rise
from the weeds ('Dormuit non mortua est')
and stand clutching at elder branches to prop
her dizzy bones after centuries of sleep?

The nettles, in fact, have also been removed:
a kind man with a spade has just slain them
so that I could kneel on the earth and scan
the truths, half-truths and guesses on her stone.

'Here lie the earthy remains' (I like 'earthy')
'of Ann the wife of Henry King'; then (huge
letters) 'Gentleman'. Not quite, I think:
it was his children who cried out their rank.

Henry was a grazier in his will;
but Anne, his lady, brought him eighty acres
and a fading touch of class; then lived so long
they buried a legend here – her age is wrong.

Homage (or weariness) called her 95,
adding perhaps five years. Her birth's gone under
the rubble of time, just as her grave was lost
when the church expanded a few yards to the east.

But I know who she was. I've traced her lineage
through wills and marriage bonds until I know it
better than she herself may have done, poor dear,
having outlived her age. And yes, she's here:

I've brought her with me. As I stroke the stone
with hands related to hers, I can feel
the charge transmitted through eight steps
of generations. She's at my fingertips.


# Beanfield

Somehow you've driven fifty miles to stand
in a beanfield, on the bumpy ridges
at the edge of it, not among the blossom
but under the larks – you can hear but not see them;
and it's not even where the house was –
the house, you think, was under the airfield
(beanfield, airfield, ploughed field) –
they ploughed the house but left the twitter of larks,
a pins-and-needles aerial tingling;
yet somehow this, you're sure, is Frances St John.
How do you know? It just is.
She's here; she's not here; she was once.
The larks are other larks' descendants.
Four hundred years. It feels like a kind of love.


# Ancestor to Devotee

What are you loving me with? I'm dead.
What gland of tenderness throbs in you,
yearning back through the silt of ages
to a face and a voice you never knew?

When you find my name in a document
or my signature on a will,
what is it that makes you hold your breath –
what reverent, half-perverted thrill?

'Flesh of my flesh,' we could call each other;
but not uniquely: I've hundreds more
in my posterity, and for you
unreckoned thousands have gone before.

What's left of me, if you gathered it up,
is a faggot of bones, some ink-scrawled paper,
flown-away cells of skin and hair...
you could set the lot on fire with a taper.

You breathe your scorching filial love
on a web of related facts and a name.
But I'm combustible now. Watch out:
you'll burn me up with that blow-torch flame.


# Frances


Her very hand. Her signature –
upright, spiky, jagged with effort –
or his hand on hers, was it,
her son's grasp locked on her knuckles?

'F. Weale'. Third of her surnames.
*I Frances Weale of Arlesey,*
*widowe, being weake in body*
*but of perfecte memory,*

*doe make this my last will*
*in the yeare 1638...*
*Item I give to my sonne Samuell Browne*
*my halfe dozen of silver spoones...*

\*

They've had quite a history, those spoons.
My first husband bequeathed them to my second –
or at least to his mother, Goodwife Weale:
'one haulfe dozen of silver spoones
which are alone and seldom occupied' –
little guessing they'd come back to me.

248

I was supposed to go away quietly
and live at Ashby Mill in Lincolnshire,
there to 'rest myself contented' and not
(repeat *not* – he did go on about it)
sue for my thirds, my widow's right in law.
Nicholas wasn't one for women's rights.

I was to have the bringing up of Samuel,
our older son; but John, our younger boy,
was to stay behind with the man Nicholas called
his 'trustie frende', Thomas Weale of Polebrook,
his joint executor. I was to be the other –
as long as I didn't claim my thirds, of course.

I was to keep the buildings in repair;
I wasn't to fell any of the trees...
he was going to rule us all from beyond the grave,
my iron rod of a husband, Nicholas Browne,
BA, BD, Rector of Polebrook, Prebendary
of Peterborough Cathedral; puritan.

Well, I wouldn't be ruled. I was done with that.
I'd had eleven years of being meek.
So when he tried to shunt me off up north
to the dull retreat he'd set aside for me
(such a fiddly, scholar's will), I didn't go.
I stayed at home and married Thomas Weale.

Yes, I know I was taking another master,
but this time I was doing it by choice;
and believe me if I tell you he was different –
a yeoman, not a cleric; less cold;
and, above all, my little John's guardian.
By marrying Thomas I kept both my children.

We made an execution of the will
to our joint satisfaction, I and Thomas
(I was still young, remember). We did our duties –
to Nicholas's estate, and to the boys
(we had no other children), and to each other.
Thomas Weale was a 'trustie frende' to us all.

No nagging about thirds when his time came:
he left me both his houses, and some land
(for my life-time only – but even a man, I think,
needs little land when he's dead), and his goods and plate.
Of which to my son John my silver bowl,
to his wife my silver cup; and the spoons to Samuel.

*In witnes whereof I have set to*
*my hande the day & yeare above written...*

\*

F. Weale. Her final signature.
Her own fingers twitching across
this very page. Not John's hand –
he wasn't there. Not clever Samuel's –

his legal glibness would have made
a brisker job of it. The wobbling
jabs of the quill are hers, an image
of weakness spelling out her strength.


## At Great Hampden

That can't be it –
not with cherubs.
After all, they were Puritans.

All the ones on the walls are too late –
too curlicued, ornate, rococo –
17th century at least.

Well, then, says the vicar,
it will be under the carpets:
a brass.

He strips off his surplice,
then his cassock,
hardly ruffling his white hair.

He rolls the strip of red carpet;
I roll the underfelt.
It sheds fluff.

A brass with figures appears. Not them.
Another. Not them.
We've begun at the wrong end.

Room for one more? Yes.
There, just in front of the altar,
a chaste plaque and a chaste coat of arms.

It says what the book says:
'Here lieth the body of Griffith Hampden...
and of Ann...' No need to write it down.

Now we begin again, the vicar and I,
rolling the carpet back,
our heads bent to the ritual;

tweaking and tidying the heavy edges
we move our arms in reciprocal gestures
like women folding sheets in a launderette.

A button flips off someone's jacket.
Yours? I offer it to the vicar.
No, yours. He hands it back with a bow.


## At Baddesley Clinton


A splodge of blood on the oak floor
in the upstairs parlour, near the hearth.

Nicholas Brome splashed it here
five centuries ago, the villain.

Not his blood; he kept his,
apart from what he handed down

(drops of it circulating still
in my own more law-abiding veins).

It was a priest's blood he squirted:
out with his sword and stuck it into

the local parson, whom he caught
'chockinge his wife under ye chinne'.

Not the same class of murder
as when he ambushed his father's killer.


251

That was cold blood at the crossroads;
hot blood in the parlour's different.

But he got the King's and the Pope's pardons,
and built the church a new west tower.

There it stands among the bluebells:
'NICHOLAS BROME ESQVIRE LORD OF

BADDESLEY DID NEW BVILD THIS STEEPLE
IN THE RAIGNE OF KING HENRY THE SEAVENTH.'

His other memorial was more furtive;
it trickled down under the rushes

and stayed there. Easy to cover it up,
but more fun now for the tourists

to see it crying out his crime.
It *is* blood: they've analysed it.

On some surfaces, in some textures,
blood's indelible, they say.


# Traitors

> '... *For that preposterous sinne wherein he did offend,*
> *In his posteriour parts had his preposterous end.'*
> MICHAEL DRAYTON: *Poly-Olbion*
> (on Edward II, murdered by Roger de Mortimer, 1327)


Naughty ancestors, I tell them,
baby-talking my cosy family –
the history ones, the long-ago
cut-out figures I've found in books.

Cut up, too, a few of them: quartered –
you, for instance, regicide
who cuddled a king's wife, and then
had her husband done away with.

You never touched him yourself, of course;
but wasn't it your own vision,
to roger him to death like that,
a red-hot poker up his rear?

Well, he had it coming to him,
you might have sneered (I see you sneering:
a straight man, in that you preferred
women to Eddy-Teddy-bears).

It's never only about sex.
Power, as usual, was the hormone;
and two of those who had the power
were my other naughties, the Despensers.

It wasn't Hugh the king's playmate
but Hugh his father who begat us,
through a less blatant son. Both Hughs
lost their balls before the scaffold.

That was how the sequence went,
for treason: chop, then hang, then quarter.
So fell all three. Only the king
died without a mark on his body –

or so they say. It's all hearsay.
Perhaps the king and Hugh the younger
were just good friends; perhaps the murder
wasn't a murder; perhaps the blood

of traitors isn't in my veins,
but just the blood of ambitious crooks
with winning Anglo-Norman accents
and risky tastes in sex. Perhaps.

Blood must be in it somewhere, though;
I see them bundled into a box,
dismembered toys, still faintly squeaking,
one with royal blood on his paws.

# Swings and Roundabouts

My ancestors are creeping down from the north –
from Lancashire and the West Riding,
from sites all over Leicestershire,

down through the Midlands; from their solid outpost
in Lincolnshire, and their halts in Rutland,
down through Northants and Beds and Bucks.

They're doing it backwards, through the centuries:
from the Industrial Revolution
they're heading south, past the Enclosures

and the Civil War, through Elizabethan times
to the dissolution of the monasteries,
the Wars of the Roses, and beyond.

From back-to-backs in Manchester they glide
in reverse to stocking-frames in Syston,
from there back to their little farms,

then further back to grander premises,
acquiring coats of arms and schooling
in their regression to higher things.

They're using the motorways; they're driving south
in their armour or their ruffs and doublets
along the M1 and the A1.

They've got as far as the South Mimms roundabout.
A little group in merchants' robes
is filtering through London, aiming

for a manor-house and lands in Chislehurst
across the road from a school I went to;
and somewhere round about Footscray

they'll meet me riding my bike with Lizzie Wood
when I was twelve; they'll rush right through me
and blow the lot of us back to Domesday.

# Peter Wentworth in Heaven

The trees have all gone from the grounds of my manor –
the plums, quinces, close-leaved pears –
where I walked in the orchard, planning my great speech;
and the house gone too. No matter.

My *Pithie Exhortation* still exists –
go and read it in your British Library.
I have discussed it here with your father;
he was always a supporter of free speech.

The trouble it brought me it is not in my nature
to regret. Only for my wife I grieved:
she followed me faithfully into the Tower;
her bones lie there, in St Peter ad Vincula.

I would not have gone home to Lillingstone Lovell,
if my friends had gained my release, without her,
'my chiefest comfort in this life, even
the best wife that ever poor gentleman enjoyed'.

She was a Walsingham; her subtle brother
was the Queen's man; he guarded his own back.
Any fellow-feeling he may once have cherished
for our cause he strangled in his bosom.

I was too fiery a Puritan for him.
His wife remembered mine in her will:
'to my sister Wentworthe a payre of sables'.
Not so Francis: he was no brother to us.

Well, we are translated to a different life,
my loyal Elizabeth and I.
We walk together in the orchards of Heaven –
a place I think you might find surprising.

But then you found me surprising too
when you got some notion of me, out of books.
Read my *Exhortation*, and my *Discourse*;
so you may understand me when we come to meet.

238-39: **Mary Derry** married William Eggington in 1800 and was the great-great-grandmother of Samuel Adcock's wife Eva Eggington.

240: **Moses Lambert: the facts:** Moses Lambert, 1821-1868, was the father of Mary Ellen Lambert (not the premarital baby in this poem but a later child), who married William Henry Eggington and was the mother of Eva.

240-41: **Samuel Joynson** was Amelia Joynson's brother.

241: **Amelia:** Amelia Joynson, 1847-1899, married John Adcock, 1842-1911, and was Samuel Adcock's mother.

242: **Barber:** John Adcock, 1874-1895, was the son of John and Amelia, and brother of Sam Adcock.

246-47: **Anne Welby** married Henry King, 1680-1756. Their granddaughter Elizabeth King married William Adcock, 1737-1814, Samuel Adcock's great-great-grandfather.

247, 248-50: **Beanfield** and **Frances:** Frances St John married Nicholas Browne, rector of Polebrook, Northants, in 1597, and was Anne Welby's great-great-grandmother.

250-51: **At Great Hampden:** Griffith Hampden, 1543-1591, and his wife Anne Cave were the parents of Mary Hampden who married Walter Wentworth, son of Peter. Their daughter Mary Wentworth married John Browne; these were the great-grandparents of Anne Welby.

251-52, 252-53: **At Baddesley Clinton** and **Traitors:** These assorted villains figure in the family tree of Elizabeth Ferrers, mother of Griffith Hampden. Baddesley Clinton is in Warwickshire; the house belongs to the National Trust.

255: **Peter Wentworth in Heaven:** Peter Wentworth, MP, 1524-1597, was imprisoned in the Tower of London several times by Elizabeth I for demanding that Parliament should be free to discuss the succession and other matters without interference. His wife Elizabeth Walsingham died in 1596 in the Tower. Her sister-in-law who mentioned Elizabeth in her will was Sir Francis Walsingham's first wife, Anne.

## II

## Tongue Sandwiches

Tongue sandwiches on market-day
in the King's Head Hottle (I could read;
my sister couldn't.) Always the same
for lunch on market-day in Melton.

No sign of a bottle in the hottle –
or not upstairs in the dining-room;
the bottles were in the room below,
with the jolly farmers around the door.

I didn't know we were in a pub,
or quite what pubs were: Uncle managed
to be a not unjolly farmer
with only tea to loosen his tongue.

And what did I think 'tongue' was?
These rose-pink slices wrapped in bread?
Or the slithery-flappy tube behind
my milk-teeth, lapping at novelties

(yes, of course I'd heard of 'ho-*tells*')
and syphoning up Midlands vowels
to smother my colonial whine?
(Something new for Mummy and Daddy,

coming to visit us at Christmas,
these local 'oohs' and 'ahs', as in
'Moommy, there's blood in the lavatory!
Soombody moost have killed a rabbit.')

On the way back to Uncle's cart
(how neat that his name was George Carter!)
we passed the beasts in the cattle-stalls –
their drooling lips, their slathering tongues.

The horse was a safer kind of monster,
elephant-calm between the shafts
as Auntie and Uncle loaded up
and we all piled on. Then bumpety-bump

along the lanes. I was impatient
for *Jerry of St Winifred's* –
my Sunday School prize, my first real book
that wasn't babyish with pictures –

to curl up with it in the armchair
beside the range, for my evening ration:
'Only a chapter a day,' said Auntie.
'Too much reading's bad for your eyes.'

I stuck my tongue out (not at her –
in a trance of concentration), tasting
the thrilling syllables: 'veterinary
surgeon', 'papyrus', 'manuscript'.

Jerry was going to be a vet;
so when she found the injured puppy
and bandaged its paw with her handkerchief,
and the Squire thanked her – well, you could see!

As for me, when I sat for hours
writing a story for Mummy and Daddy,
and folded the pages down the middle
to make a book, I had no ambition.


## The Pilgrim Fathers


I got a Gold Star for the Pilgrim Fathers,
my first public poem, when I was nine.
I think I had to read it out to the class;
but no one grilled me about it, line by line;

no one asked me to expatiate on
my reasons for employing a refrain;
no one probed into my influences,
or said 'Miss Adcock, perhaps you could explain

your position as regards colonialism.
Here you are, a New Zealander in Surrey,
describing the exportation of new values
to America. Does this cause you any worry?

And what about the title, 'Pilgrim Fathers' –
a patriarchal expression, you'll agree –
how does it relate to the crucial sentence
in stanza one: 'Nine children sailed with we'?

Were you identifying with your age-group?
Some of us have wondered if we detect
a growing tendency to childism
in your recent poems. Might this be correct?'

No one even commented on the grammar –
it didn't seem important at the time.
I liked the sound of it, is all I'd have said
if they'd questioned me. I did it for the rhyme.


## Paremata

Light the Tilley lamp:
I want to write a message,
while the tide laps the slipway
and someone else cooks sausages.

Make the Primus hiss:
twizzley music. Dusk time.
Bring back the greeds of childhood;
forget young love and all that slime.


## Camping

When you're fifteen, no one understands you.
And why had I been invited, anyway? –
On a camping holiday with my Latin teacher
and her young friends, two men in their twenties.
I didn't understand them, either.

The one I fancied was the tall one
with soft brown eyes. He was a hairdresser.
One day the Primus toppled over
and a pan of water scalded his foot.

The skin turned into soggy pink crêpe paper –
grisly; but it gave him a romantic limp
and a lot of sympathy.
Once he condescended to lean on my shoulder
for a few steps along a wooded path.
Next time I offered, he just laughed.

Funnily enough, two days later
I scalded my own foot: not badly,
but as badly as I dared.
                              It didn't work.
Everyone understood me perfectly.


## Bed and Breakfast


They thought he looked like Gregory Peck, of course;
and they thought I looked like Anne somebody –
a name I vaguely recognised: no one special,
not Greer Garson or Vivien Leigh.
What they really must have thought I looked like
was young. But they were being kind;
and anyway, we'd asked for separate rooms.

When it was late enough, Gregory Peck
came into mine – or did I go into his?
Which of us tiptoed along the passage
in our pyjamas? And to do what?
                              Not sex,
but what you did when you weren't quite doing sex.
It made you a bit sticky and sweaty,
but it didn't make you pregnant,
and you didn't actually have to know anything.
You didn't even take off your pyjamas.

Unfortunately since it never got anywhere
it went on most of the night. No sleep.
At breakfast, though, I can't have looked too haggard:
Gregory Peck was not put off.
For that I could thank the resilience of youth –
one of the very few advantages,
as far as I could see, of that hateful condition.
Anne Whatsit might have looked worse;
but then I suppose she'd have had makeup.

# Rats

That was the year the rats got in:
always somebody at the back door
clutching a half-dozen of beer,
asking if we felt like a game of darts.

Then eyes flickering away from the dartboard
to needle it out. What were we up to?
Were we really all living together –
three of us? Four of us? Who was whose?

And what about the children? What indeed.
We found a real rat once, dead
on the wash-house floor. Not poison:
old age, perhaps, or our old cat.

We buried the corpse. Our own victims
were only our reputations, we thought –
bright-eyed with panic and bravado.
It can take thirty years to find out.


# Stockings

The first transvestite I ever went to bed with
was the last, as far as I know.
It was in the 60s, just before tights.
He asked if he could put my stockings on –
on me, I thought; on him, it turned out.
His legs weren't much of a shape,
and my suspender-belt was never the same
after he'd strained it round his middle.
But apart from that, things could have been worse.
The whisky helped.

I never went out with him again;
and I never, ever, told his secret –
who'd want to? (He must have counted on
the inhibiting power of embarrassment.)
But I still went to his parties.
At one of them I met Yoko Ono.

# A Political Kiss

In the dream I was kissing John Prescott –
or about to kiss him; our eyes had locked
and we were leaning avidly forward,
lips out-thrust, certain protuberances
under our clothing brushing each other's fronts,
when my mother saw us, and I woke up.

In fact I've never kissed an MP.
The nearest I got was a Labour peer
in a telephone box at Euston station
(one of the old red kiosks –
which seemed appropriate at the time).
But I don't suppose that counts, does it?


# An Apology

Can it be that I was unfair
to Tony Blair?
His teeth, after all, are beyond compare;
but does he take too much care
over his hair?

If he were to ask me out for a meal,
how would I feel?
Would I grovel and kneel,
aflame with atavistic socialist zeal?
No, I'm sorry, he doesn't appeal:
he's not quite real.

In the House he sounds sincere,
but over a candlelit table, I fear,
his accents wouldn't ring sweetly in my ear.
Oh dear.

I'd love to see him in No. 10,
but he doesn't match my taste in men.

# Festschrift

Dear So-and-so, you're seventy. Well done!
Or is it sixty? It's a bit confusing
remembering which, of all my ageing friends,
is the one about whose talents I'm enthusing.

I'm getting on myself, a fact which makes one
occasionally vague – as you may know,
having achieved such venerable status;
although in you, of course, the years don't show.

Anyway, I'm delighted to contribute
to the memorial volume which your wife –
or publisher – is secretly arranging
to mark this splendid milestone in your life.

As one of your most passionate admirers
I'm glad to tell the world of my conviction
that you've transformed the course of literature
by your poetry – or do I mean your fiction?

Oh dear. Well, never mind. Congratulations,
from a near contemporary, on your weighty
achievements; and you'll hear this all again
in ten years' time, at seventy – sorry! eighty.


# Offerings

A garland for Dame Propinquity, goddess
of work-places, closed circles and small towns,
who let our paths cross and our eyes meet
so many times in the course of duty
that we became each other's pleasure, and every
humdrum encounter a thundering in the veins.
We place at the hem of her fluted marble robe
this swag of meadow flowers, picked nearby,
as much a bribe as a thank-offering,
asking her to smile on our extensions
and elaborations of what she began.

And now, to be on the safe side, a recherché
confection of orchids and newly hybridised lilies
for her sister, Lady Novelty: not to leave us.

263

# Danger: Swimming and Boating Prohibited

This tender 'V' of thighs below my window
is one end of Kuba's mother,
sprawled for the May sun in her bikini.
I hardly know her face. 'Ku-baah!' she calls,
and scolds him drowsily in Polish.

Kuba's off with his bikie friends,
the big boys, old enough for school.
'Ku-baah!' they shout. Their accent's perfect.
They bump their tyres in circles over the grass,
towards and then away from the glinting water.

In winter, I'm told, the swans come up
and tap their beaks on the windows, begging.
Today a lone brown female mallard
waddles quacking forlorn parodies
of a person doing duck imitations.

Kuba tries to run her down.
She flaps off, squawking, back to the Broad.
It's a rough male world down there;
the drakes are playing football hooligans,
dunking each other, shamming rape –

well, what else is there to do
while their sober mates are hatching eggs?
Only one brood's appeared so far.
I count the ducklings every day:
eight, five, four, still four (good!), three...

I'll go and check again in a minute.
'Grow up!' I'll tell them. 'Hang on in there!'
Downstairs the front end of Kuba's mother,
a streaked blonde top-knot, pokes out of a window.
'Kuba!' she calls again. 'Ku-baah!'

# Risks

When we heard the results of our tests
we felt rather smug (if worried);
we said to each other loudly in public
'Well, that's it for space-travel;
we mustn't go up there again.
We can't afford to be bombarded
with any more radiation, dammit!'

No more risks: that was the policy.
In which case what are we doing here
scrambling along this rocky gorge
with hardly a finger-hold to bless us,
and the bridge down, and a train coming,
and the river full of crocodiles?
(I think I invented the crocodiles.)


# Blue Footprints in the Snow

But there's no snow yet: the footprints
are made by a rubber stamp, a toy
I daren't give to a child. (Warning:
'Ink not guaranteed to wash out.')

First the gale, and now the rain,
and soon the sleet, and then the footprints.

The TV weather map is stamped
with rows of identical cloud-shapes,
each dangling two white crystals
and striding briskly south from Scotland.

But the feet are close together, jumping
kangaroo-hops on a white page.

We thought we were stuck on Crusoe's island,
marooned in summer, dry and stranded
under clouds that would come to nothing –
or nothing anyone could want.

Earth-based, earth-bound, paper-bound,
we had to play with toy footprints.

Now, though, prophetic silhouettes
emerge from a computer to bless us.
The clouds leap up; the crystals fall
and multiply on roofs and gardens.

The feet are lifting off the page
to bite blue shadows into the snow.


## Summer in Bucharest


We bought raspberries in the market;
but raspberries are discredited:

they sag in their bag, fermenting
into a froth of suspect juice.

And strawberries are seriously compromised:
a taint – you must have heard the stories.

As for redcurrants, well, they say
the only real redcurrants are dead.

(Don't you believe it: the fields are full of them,
swelling hopefully on their twigs,

and the dead ones weren't red anyway
but some mutation of black or white.)

We thought of choosing gooseberries,
until we heard they'd been infiltrated

by raspberries in gooseberry jackets.
You can't tell what to trust these days.

There are dates, they say, but they're imported;
and it's still too early for the grape harvest.

All we can do is wait and hope.
It's been a sour season for fruit.

*1990*

# Moneymore

Looked better last time, somehow, on a wet weekday
from under an umbrella – rain
blurring my lens and rinsing the handsome faces
of the Drapers' Company buildings, lights on early,
golden glimmers in puddles, cars growling
at each other over parking spaces –

than on this mild and spacious Sunday afternoon,
no car but ours parked in the High Street
by the painted kerbstones – white, blue, red, white, blue,
with lads loafing in front of the Orange Hall
and an old woman, daft in the sunshine,
greeting strangers: 'How *are* you? How are *you?*'

Oh, yes, and that parked van outside the Market House...
but time's up; I've a plane to catch.
If we take the Ballyronan road
we shan't see Magherafelt, a town I've always
wanted to visit; where ten hours from now
another van will discharge its sudden load.

# The Voices

The voices change on the answering-machines:
not the friend but the friend's widow;
not the friend but the other friend.

'I'm not here' the machine tells you.
'This is the job I never did –
this fluent interface with the world.

He/she did it; but I'm learning.
Now all the jobs are mine or no one's.
There's no one here. Leave a message.'

# Willow Creek

The janitor came out of his eely cave
and said 'Your mother was a good swimmer.
Go back and tell her it's not yet time.'

Were there no other animals in Eden?
When she dives under the roots, I thought,
an eel is the last shape she'll want to meet.

Her brother was the one for eels: farm-wise,
ruthless about food. You roll the skin back
and pull it off inside out like a stocking.

He grew up with dogs, horses and cattle.
She was more at home with water and music;
there were several lives for her after the creek.

In one of them she taught my younger son
to swim in the Greek sea; and walked through Athens
under a parasol, to buy us melon.

Fruit for the grandchildren; nectarines and pears
for the great-grandchildren; feijoa-parties...
'There's more of that to come,' said the janitor.

'But no more swimming. Remember how she plunged
into a hotel pool in bra and knickers,
rather than miss the chance? She must have been sixty.'

I had some questions for the janitor,
but he submerged himself under the willows
in his cavern where I couldn't follow –

you have to be invited; I wasn't, yet,
and neither was she. Meanwhile, she's been allowed
a rounded segment of something warm and golden:

not pomegranate, paw-paw. She used to advise
eating the seeds: a few of them, with the fruit,
were good for you in some way – I forget.

Long life, perhaps. She knows about these things.
And she won't let a few eels bother her.
She's tougher than you might think, my mother.

# Giggling

I mustn't mention the hamster's nose –
it sets you off. You giggle like Auntie Lizzie
forty-odd years old, when she was your age:
heading for ninety. Great gigglers,
you and your mother and your aunt.
They were white-haired and well-padded;
you were too skinny for a mother,
we thought, with our teenage angst,
afraid of turning into you.

'It just struck me funny,' said Auntie Lizzie,
' – that old drunk in his coffin
with all those flowers. I got the giggles.'
Her comfortable shoulders heaved
as yours do, now that you're her shape.
She lived to a hundred and three,
blind and deaf at the end, but not to be fooled:
when her daughter died, she knew.
I hope you'll be spared that extremity.

Of course it wasn't the hamster's nose:
that's just shorthand. It was the fireman's;
he'd given it the kiss of life,
and the hamster... oh, well, never mind –
you know the story. You're off again.
I never guessed old age was so much fun.


# Trio

Julia has chocolate on her chin,
and isn't getting far with the cut-out stick
they've given her as a bow. It doesn't matter;
the music's there, behind her serious eyes.

Lily's in her knickers and a sweater
passed down from Oliver, who hated it,
her shiny hair glinting above her shiny
half-sized (or is it quarter-sized?) violin.

Oliver's playing his cello: he knows how;
and that's not all he knows about: he made
the cardboard fiddle – bridge and strings and struts
and curves, a three-dimensional miracle

of Sellotaping – for Julia to play at
playing like Lily, and for family harmony.
Soon, after her birthday, when she's four,
she'll have Suzuki lessons and the real thing.


## The Video


When Laura was born, Ceri watched.
They all gathered around Mum's bed –
Dad and the midwife and Mum's sister
and Ceri. 'Move over a bit,' Dad said –
he was trying to focus the camcorder
on Mum's legs and the baby's head.

After she had a little sister,
and Mum had gone back to being thin,
and was twice as busy, Ceri played
the video again and again.
She watched Laura come out, and then,
in reverse, she made her go back in.

# NEW POEMS

(2000)

# Easter

On the curved staircase he embraced me.
'You've got a ladybird in your hair.
Without hurting it, come closer,'
one of us said, in a daze of dream.

But I thought we were in Jerusalem?
– That is indeed the name of this city.
It would be difficult to wind down further
below the ground than to this cave of birth.

All the best dreams have a baby in them.
Year after year I give birth to my son.
Clutch him in his blanket, close in your arms;
the chill from the walls burns colder than marble.

*30 March 1997*


# High Society

Here, children, are the pastel 50s for you:
everything, even to Bing Crosby's trousers,
is powder-blue – if it isn't petal-pink,
like Grace Kelly's cashmere sweater.

The name of the song is 'True Love'.
We may have crooned it over your cradles.
The name of the age was 'Innocence Incorporated'.
We bought it, along with the first LPs.

Why do you thing we turned out as we did? –
We, your parents, that is. You turned out OK:
you didn't have to rebel against it;
you were only just being conceived.

We dressed you in pink or blue,
popped nipples into your mouths (we were big on breast-feeding),
and cigarettes into our own (same thing),
then went to the next party. The jazz was good.

Now you're rebelling against our rebellions.
You haven't been married as often as us.
Your kids have shrugged and taken to computers.
We worry about them; it's what we do these days.

Our parents worried about our divorces
(so Hollywood!) and then embarked on their own.
But we've had enough of Technicolor;
after all, we were conceived in black and white.


## For Meg
*(i.m. Meg Sheffield, 1940-1997)*


Half the things you did were too scary for me.
Skiing? No thanks. Riding? I've never learnt.
Canoeing? I'd be sure to tip myself out
and stagger home, ignominiously wet.
It was my son, that time in Kathmandu,
who galloped off with you to the temple at Bodnath
in a monsoon downpour, both of you on horses
from the King of Nepal's stables. Not me.

And as for the elephants – my God, the elephants!
How did you get me up on to one of those?
First they lay down; the way to climb aboard
was to walk up a gross leg, then straddle a sack
(that's all there was to sit on), while the creature
wobbled and swayed through the jungle for slow hours.
It felt like riding on the dome of St Paul's
in an earthquake. This was supposed to be a treat.

You and Alex and Maya, in her best sari,
sat beaming at the wildlife, you with your camera
proficiently clicking. You were pregnant at the time.
I clung with both hot hands to the bit of rope
that was all there was to cling to. The jungle steamed.
As soon as we were back in sight of the camp
I got off and walked through a river to reach it.
You laughed, but kindly. We couldn't all be like you.

Now you've done the scariest thing there is;
and all the king's horses, dear Meg, won't bring you back.

# A Visiting Angel

My angel's wearing dressing-up clothes –
her sister's ballet-skirt, her mother's top,
some spangles, a radiant smile.

She looks as if she might take off
and float in the air – whee! But of course
you've guessed: she's not an angel really.

Her screeches when you try to dress her
make the neighbours think of child abuse.
She has to be in the mood for clothes.

Once, for the sake of peace, when she wouldn't even
part with her soggy night-time nappy,
I took her to the shops in her pyjamas.

And what about the shoe she left on the train?
But then she sat like Cinderella,
serene and gracious, trying on the new ones.

Has she been spoilt? Her big sister,
no less pretty, gave up the cuteness contest
and settled for being the sensible one.

It's tough being sister to an angel
(a burden I bore for years myself),
but being an angel's grandmother is bliss.

I want to buy her French designer outfits.
Madness. It would be cheaper and more fun
to go to Paris. So we all do that.

A special deal on Eurostar.
Halfway there, she comes to sit beside me
on Daddy's knee, and stares into my face.

'Fleur,' she says thoughtfully, 'I love you.'
Wow! That's angel-talk, no doubt of it.
Where can I buy her a halo and some wings?

# It's Done This!

*(for Mia, Kristen and Marilyn)*

Help! It's hidden my document,
and when I try to get it back,
tells me it's already in use.
It keeps changing the names of my files.
Why won't the Edit Menu appear?
It takes no notice of me. Help!

'You have made changes which alter
the global template, Normal. Do you
want to save them?' Oh, please, no –
what have I altered? The ozone layer?
Help! But Help refuses to help;
the message goes on glaring at me.

There are some things you can't cancel –
or, if you have, you wish you hadn't.
'This may damage your computer.'
What may? 'Windows is closing down.'
But Windows isn't. Who can I ring
to rescue me, at nearly midnight?

Somehow, between us, we survive,
even though I've lost page 4
and all the margins have gone crazy.
What if I've bought the wrong scanner?
What if my printer's rather slow?
I'm getting rather slow myself.

It's nearly midnight once again,
and Windows isn't closing down –
nor do I want it to, just yet.
We're in it together. So be it.
I'll sit here, at the end of an age,
and wait for the great roll-over.

# Kensington Gardens

## Droppings

Poetry for the summer. It comes out blinking
from hibernation, sniffs at pollen and scents,
and agrees to trundle around with me, for as long
as the long days last, digesting what we discover
and now and then extruding a little package of words.

## Poetry Placement

They suggest I hold court in the Queen's Temple
(hoping it doesn't smell of urine).
Too exposed, I say; no doors or windows.
We settle for a room by the Powder Store (1805):
where else should poets meet but in a magazine?

## Peter Pan

What was the creepiest thing about him?
The callousness? The flitting with fairies?
The detachable shadow? No,
that feature that was most supposed to entrance you:
the 'little pearls' of his never-shed milk-teeth.

## The Fairies' Winter Palace

Queen Caroline, I think, planted these chestnuts
with their spiralling ridged bark. In another world
Peter and his freaky friends claimed this hollow one,
capacious enough for several children, if they dare,
to stand inside, holding their breath. Don't try it!

*Heron*

A seagull on every post but one;
on the nearest post a heron.
Is he asleep? Stuffed, nailed to his perch?
He hunches a scornful shoulder, droops
an eyelid. Find out, fish!


*Handful*

Now that there are no sparrows
what I feel landing on my outstretched hand
with a light skitter of claws
to snatch up a peanut and whirl off
are the coloured substitutes: great tits, blue tits.


*Jay*

A crow in fancy dress
tricked out in pink and russet
with blue and black and white accessories
lurks in a tree, managing not to squawk
his confession: 'I am not a nice bird.'

\*

*Sandy*

A cold day, for July, by the Serpentine.
She brings us up to date on her melanoma:
some capillary involvement, this time.
Just here is where her grandparents first met.
She still hopes to finish her family history.

\*

277

## Aegithalos Caudatus

Don't think I didn't see you in the apple tree,
three of you, hanging out with the gang, your long tails
making the other tits look docked; and in the roses –
all that dangling upside-down work – feeding, I hope,
on aphids. Come any time. My garden's all yours.

*

## Birthday Card

This Winifred Nicholson card for my mother's birthday,
because she loves Winifred Nicholson's work –
or did, when she had her wits. Now, if all that's forgotten,
she may at least perhaps like it, each new time
it strikes her: 'That's nice... That's nice... That's nice.'

*

## Polypectomy

'You need a bolster,' said the nurse, strapping a roll
of gauze under my nose, when my dressings threatened
to bleed into my soup. I sat up in bed
insinuating the spoon under my bloody moustache
and crowing internally: after all that, real life.

## Butterfly Food

The Monarch caterpillars were crawling away,
having stripped bare the only plant they could fancy.
We raced to the Garden Centre for two more,
and decked them with stripy dazzlers – lucky to have hatched
in NZ and not in the GM USA.

## Checking Out

In my love affair with the natural world
I plan to call quits before it all turns sour:
before the last thrush or the last skylark,
departing, leaves us at each other's throats,
I intend to be bone-meal, scattered.

## Goodbye

Goodbye, summer. Poetry goes to bed.
The scruffy blue tits by the Long Water are fed
for the last time from my palm – with cheese, not bread
(more sustaining). The chestnut blossoms are dead.
The gates close early. What wanted to be said is said.

# Index of titles and first lines

(Titles are shown in italics, first lines in roman type.)

Abandoning all my principles, 82
*Accidental*, 89
*Accidents*, 177
A cold day, for July, by the Serpentine, 277
*Acris Hiems*, 74
*Across the Moor*, 142
A crow in fancy dress, 277
*A Day in October*, 105
*Advice to a Discarded Lover*, 29
*Aegithalos Caudatus*, 278
After they had not made love, 40
*Afterwards*, 40
*Against Coupling*, 49
*A Game*, 34
A garland for Dame Propinquity, goddess, 263
*A Haunting*, 243
*A Hymn to Friendship*, 214
Air-raid shelters at school were damp tunnels, 169
A letter from that pale city, 74
All my dead people, 76
All my scars are yours. We talk of pledges, 18
All the flowers have gone back into the ground, 25
Already I know my way around the bazaar, 80
*Aluminium*, 213
*Amelia*, 241
*A Message*, 89
Among the Roman love-poets, possession, 14
*An Apology*, 262
*Ancestor to Devotee*, 247
*An Emblem*, 137
*An Epitaph*, 176
Angry Mozart: the only kind for now, 129
*An Illustration to Dante*, 77
*Anne Welby*, 246
Another poem about a Norfolk church, 90
*A Political Kiss*, 262
A postcard from my father's childhood, 195
Arranging for my due ration of terror, 94
A seagull on every post but one, 277
As if the week had begun anew, 204
A small dazzle of stained glass which, 157
A snail is climbing up the window-sill, 21
A splodge of blood on the oak floor, 251
*A Surprise in the Peninsula*, 38
*At Baddesley Clinton*, 251
*At Great Hampden*, 250
At Moa Point that afternoon, 64

*At the Creative Writing Course*, 92
*A Visiting Angel*, 274
*A Walk in the Snow*, 105
A wall of snuffling snouts in close-up, 201
*A Way Out*, 87

*Barber*, 242
*Beanfield*, 247
*Beauty Abroad*, 17
*Beaux Yeux*, 94
*Bed and Breakfast*, 260
*Being Blind*, 41
Being in Mr Wood's class this time, 170
*Being Taken from the Place*, 176
*Below Loughrigg*, 118
*Bethan and Bethany*, 143
Bethan and Bethany sleep in real linen, 143
*Binoculars*, 119
*Birthday Card*, 278
*Blue Footprints in the Snow*, 265
*Blue Glass*, 143
*Bodnath*, 79
*Bogyman*, 35
Books, music, the garden, cats, 70
Boss-eye, wall-eye, squinty lid, 110
*Briddes*, 65
'Briddes' he used to call them, 65
British, more or less; Anglican, of a kind, 61
'But look at all this beauty,' 44
*Butterfly Food*, 278
But there's no snow yet: the footprints, 265

*Camping*, 259
Can it be that I was unfair, 262
Carrying still the dewy rose, 17
Caterpillars are falling on the Writers' Union, 156
*Cat's-Eye*, 110
*Cattle in Mist*, 195
*Central Time*, 206
*Checking Out*, 279
*Chippenham*, 171
*Choices*, 184
*Clarendon Whatmough*, 36
Clarendon Whatmough sits in his chair, 36
Clear is the man and of a cold life, 103
Come, literature, and salve our wounds, 209
Coming out with your clutch of postcards, 156
*Comment*, 22
*Composition for Words and Paint*, 24
*Corrosion*, 130

Counting, 192
Country Station, 48
Coupling, 204
Crab, 135
Creosote, 206

Danger: Swimming and Boating Prohibited, 264
Dear Jim, I'm using a Shakespearian form, 68
Dear posterity, it's 2 a.m., 136
Dear So-and-so, you're seventy. Well done, 263
Death by drowning drowns the soul, 174
December Morning, 75
Declensions, 123
Demonstration, 188
Discreet, not cryptic. I write to you from the garden, 89
Don't think I didn't see you in the apple tree, 278
Doom and sunshine stream over the garden, 131
Double-take, 183
Downstream, 128
Drawings, 179
Dreaming, 141
Dreamy with illness, 134
'Drink water from the hollow in the stone...', 60
Droppings, 276
Drowning, 174
Dry Spell, 100

Earlswood, 169
Easter, 272
Eat their own hair, sheep do, 182
Eclipse, 135
Elm, laburnum, hawthorn, oak, 47
Emily Brontë's cleaning the car, 203
England's Glory, 163
Excavations, 181
External Service, 80

Failing their flesh and bones we have the gatepost, 236
Fairy-tale, 92
Festschrift, 263
Feverish, 72
Finding I've walked halfway around Loughrigg, 120
Fiona's parents need her today, 212
First she made a little garden, 48
First there is the hill, 112
Flames, 242
Flight, with Mountains, 15
Flying Back, 80
Folie à Deux, 73

For a Five-Year-Old, 21
For Andrew, 21
Foreigner, 107
Forget about the school – there was one, 167
For Heidi with Blue Hair, 161
For her gravestone to have been moved is OK, 246
For Meg, 273
4 May 1979, 131
Framed, 234
Frances, 248
From the Demolition Zone, 209
Future Work, 84

Gas, 52
Gentlemen's Hairdressers, 186
Giggling, 269
Glenshane, 82
Going Back, 113
Going Out from Ambleside, 124
Goodbye, 279
Goodbye, sweet symmetry. Goodbye, sweet world, 190
Goodbye, summer. Poetry goes to bed, 279
Goslings dive in the lake, 86
Grandma, 42
Great-great-great-uncle Frances Eggington, 235

Half an hour before my flight was called, 95
Half the things you did were too scary for me, 273
Halfway Street, Sidcup, 166
Handful, 277
Happiness, 204
Happy Ending, 40
Hauntings, 28
Having No Mind for the Same Poem, 98
He gurgled beautifully on television, 132
He had followed her across the moor, 142
He is lying on his back watching a kestrel, 124
He is my green branch growing in a far plantation, 44
Heliopsis Scabra, 200
He looked for it in the streets first, 240
Help! It's hidden my document, 275
Here are Paolo and Francesca, 77
Here are the ploughed fields of Middle England, 202
Here, children, are the pastel 50s for you, 272
Here is a hole full of men shouting, 181
Heron, 277
Her very hand. Her signature, 248
High Society, 272

His jailer trod on a rose-petal, 65
*Hotspur*, 148
*House-martins*, 200
*House-talk*, 107
How can I prove to you, 198
'Hoy!' A hand hooks me into a doorway, 243

I am in a foreign country, 81
I am sitting on the step, 45
I am the dotted lines on the map, 120
*Icon*, 178
I got a Gold Star for the Pilgrim Fathers, 258
I have made my pilgrimage a day early, 79
I have nothing to say about this garden, 20
I met an ancestor in the lane, 243
*Immigrant*, 111
I'm still too young to remember how, 177
I mustn't mention the hamster's nose, 269
*Incident*, 19
*Influenza*, 134
*In Focus*, 95
In her 1930s bob or even, perhaps, 138
*In Memoriam: James K. Baxter*, 68
In my love affair with the natural world, 279
Inside my closed eyelids, printed out, 95
*Instead of an Interview*, 115
*Instructions to Vampires*, 19
*In the Dingle Peninsula*, 108
In the dream I was kissing John Prescott, 262
In the interests of economy, 178
*In the Terai*, 108
*In the Unicorn, Ambleside*, 128
I raise the blind and sit by the window, 75
*I Ride on My High Bicycle*, 26
Is it the long dry grass that is so erotic, 88
It has to be learned afresh, 133
It is going to be a splendid summer, 84
It is not one thing, but more one thing than others, 100
It is not only the eye that is astonished, 119
*It's Done This*, 275
It's hard to stay angry with a buttercup, 197
It's the old story of the personal, 175
It was going to be a novel, 130
It was the midnight train; I was tired and edgy, 42
It went like this: I married at 22, 241
It will be typed, of course, and not all in capitals, 136
It would be rude to look out of the car windows, 210
It would not be true to say she was doing nothing, 22
I want to have ice-skates and a hoop, 128

I wish to apologise for being mangled, 176
I would not have you drain, 19
I write in praise of the solitary act, 49

*Jay*, 277
Julia has chocolate on her chin, 269
Just because it was so long ago, 237
Just visiting: another village school, 170

*Kensington Gardens*, 276
*Kilmacrenan*, 82
*Kilpeck*, 71
*Kissing*, 182
*Knife-play*, 18

*Lantern Slides*, 140
Last I became a raft of green bubbles, 128
*Last Song*, 190
Late at night we wrench open a crab, 135
*Leaving the Tate*, 156
Less like an aircraft than a kettle, 176
Let's be clear about this: I love toads, 196
*Letter from Highgate Wood*, 96
*Letter to Alistair Campbell*, 122
*Libya*, 193
Light the Tilley lamp, 259
Listen to that, 41
Literally thin-skinned, I suppose, my face, 124
*Londoner*, 116
Look, children, the wood is full of tigers, 31
Looked better last time, somehow, on a wet weekday, 267
Looking through the glass showcase, 76
*Loving Hitler*, 165

*Madmen*, 131
*Mary Derry*, 238
*Mary Magdalene and the Birds*, 145
May: autumn. In more or less recognisable, 208
*Meeting the Comet*, 222
*Mid-point*, 120
Milkmaids, buttercups, ox-eye dasies, 168
*Miss Hamilton in London*, 22
Mist like evaporating stone, 121
*Moa Point*, 64
*Moneymore*, 267
*Mornings After*, 50
*Moses Lambert: the Facts*, 240
*Mr Morrison*, 86
*Mrs Fraser's Frenzy*, 217
Mud in their beaks, the house-martins are happy, 200
My ancestors are creeping down from the north, 254
My angel's wearing dressing-up clothes, 274

My Father, 194
My great-grandfather Richey Brooks, 62
My name is Eliza Fraser, 217
My turn for Audrey Pomegranate, 172

Nature Table, 132
Naughty ancestors, I tell them, 252
Naxal, 78
Near Creeslough, 81
Neighbours lent her a tall feathery dog, 105
Nelia, 64
Nellie, 237
Neston, 170
Next Door, 199
Ngauranga Gorge Hill, 43
Nor for the same conversation again and
    again, 98
Note on Propertius, 14
Not pill-boxes, exactly: blocks, 63
November '63: eight months in London, 111
Now that there are no sparrows, 277
Nuns, now: ladies in black hoods, 166

'Oblivion, that's all. I never dream,' he said,
    141
Odd how the seemingly maddest of men, 131
Offerings, 263
Off the Track, 94
On a Son Returned to New Zealand, 44
Only a slight fever, 72
On the Border, 136
On the curved staircase he embraced me, 272
On the Land, 177
On the School Bus, 169
On the wall above the bedside lamp, 204
On the Way to the Castle, 210
Our busy springtime has corrupted, 94
Our throats full of dust, teeth harsh with it,
    108
Our Trip to the Federation, 85
Outside the National Gallery, 105

Outwood, 168
Over the Edge, 76

Paremata, 259
Parting Is Such Sweet Sorrow, 27
Pastoral, 182
Paths, 120
Paua-Shell, 110
'Personal Poem', 175
Peter Pan, 276
Peter Wentworth in Heaven, 255
Piano Concerto in E Flat Major, 138
Pink Lane, Strawberry Lane, Pudding Chare,
    141
Please Identify Yourself, 61

Poem Ended by a Death, 97
Poetry for the summer. It comes out blink-
    ing, 276
Poetry Placement, 276
Polypectomy, 278
Post Office, 187
Prelude, 88
Proposal for a Survey, 90
Pupation, 70
Purple Shining Lilies, 39

Queen Caroline, I think, planted these chest-
    nuts, 276

Rats, 261
Red-tipped, explosive, self-complete, 163
Regression, 25
Revision, 133
Richey, 62
Risks, 265
River, 109
Roles, 203
Romania, 211

St Gertrude's, Sidcup, 166
St John's School, 69
Salfords, Surrey, 167
Samuel Joynson, 240
Sandy, 277
Saturday, 45
Scalford Again, 170
Scalford School, 166
Scarcely two hours back in the country, 116
Script, 66
Sea-Lives, 110
Send-off, 95
Settlers, 112
Shakespeare's Hotspur, 132
She keeps the memory-game, 77
She'll never be able to play the piano, 222
She writes to me from a stony island, 64
Showcase, 76
Shrimping-Net, 111
Slightly frightened of the bullocks, 92
Smokers for Celibacy, 215
Snow on the tops: half the day I've sat at
    the window, 123
Somehow we manage it: to like our friends,
    214
Somehow you've driven fifty miles to stand,
    247
Some of us are a little tired of hearing that
    cigarettes kill, 215
Someone has nailed a lucky horse-shoe, 137
Somewhere in the bush, the last moa, 205
Spilt petrol, 110
Standing just under the boatshed, 111

Stepping down from the blackberry bushes, 35

*Stewart Island*, 44

*Stockings*, 261

Strange room, from this angle, 101

*Street Scene, London N2*, 185

*Street Song*, 142

*Sub Sepibus*, 245

Suddenly it's gone public; it rushed out, 211

*Summer in Bucharest*, 266

*Swings and Roundabouts*, 254

*Syringa*, 99


*Tadpoles*, 159

Tarmac, take-off: metallic words conduct us, 15

Tawny-white as a ripe hayfield, 129

That can't be it, 250

That's where they lived in the 1890s, 234

That was the year the rats got in, 261

That wet gravelly sound is rain, 70

The accidents are never happening, 177

The barber's shop has gone anonymous, 186

*The Batterer*, 203

*The Bedroom Window*, 157

The bee in the foxglove, the mouth on the nipple, 43

*The Breakfast Program*, 208

*The Bullaun*, 60

*The Chiffonier*, 158

The concrete road from the palace to the cinema, 78

*The Drought Breaks*, 70

The events of the *Aeneid* were not enacted, 39

*The Ex-Queen Among the Astronomers*, 93

*The Fairies' Winter Palace*, 276

*The Famous Traitor*, 65

*The Farm*, 212

The first spring of the new century, 238

The first transvestite I ever went to bed with, 261

The four-year-old believes he likes, 22

The French boy was sick on the floor at prayers, 166

*The Genius of Surrey*, 164

*The Greenhouse Effect*, 204

The hailstorm was in my head, 82

*The High Tree*, 173

*The Hillside*, 129

The hills, I told them; and water, and the clear air, 115

*The Inner Harbour*, 110

Their little black thread legs, their threads of arms, 159

The janitor came out of his eely cave, 268

*The Keepsake*, 162

The landscape of my middle childhood, 164

*The Last Moa*, 205

The little girls in the velvet collars, 169

*The Man Who X-Rayed an Orange*, 23

The maths master was eight feet tall, 171

The Monarch caterpillars were crawling away, 278

*The Net*, 77

Then in the end she didn't marry him, 130

The ones not in the catalogue, 179

The other option's to become a bird, 87

*The Pangolin*, 32

*The Pilgrim Fathers*, 258

The power speaks only out of sleep and blackness, 118

*The Prize-winning Poem*, 136

The queue's right out through the glass doors, 187

There are worse things than having behaved foolishly in public, 87

There have been all those tigers, of course, 32

There is no safety, 148

There they were around the wireless, 165

There was a tree higher than clouds or lightning, 173

There was never just one book for the desert island, 184

There were always the places I couldn't spell, or couldn't find on maps, 113

*The Ring*, 130

The room is full of clichés – 'Throw me a crumb', 27

*The Russian War*, 235

These coloured slopes ought to inspire, 121

These winds bully me, 107

The sheets have been laundered clean, 77

*The Soho Hospital for Women*, 101

*The Spirit of the Place*, 121

The strong image is always the river, 109

The surface dreams are easily remembered, 50

The syringa's out. That's nice for me, 99

The tadpoles won't keep still in the aquarium, 132

*The Telephone Call*, 179

*The Three-toed Sloth*, 49

The three-toed sloth is the slowest creature we know, 49

'The time is nearly one o'clock, 206

The trees have all gone from the grounds of my manor, 255

The underworld of children becomes the overworld, 143

The Vale of Grasmere, 121
The Video, 270
The Voices, 267
The voices change on the answering-
machines, 267
The Voyage Out, 62
The Wars, 244
The Water Below, 30
The weekly dietary scale, 62
The worst thing that can happen, 193
They are throwing the ball, 34
They asked me 'Are you sitting down, 179
They call it pica, 73
They give us moistened BOAC towels, 80
The young are walking on the riverbank, 182
The young cordwainer (yes, that's right), 240
They set the boy to hairdressing, 242
They serve revolving saucer eyes, 93
They suggest I hold court in the Queen's
Temple, 276
They thought he looked like Gregory Peck,
of course, 260
They will wash all my kisses and fingerprints
off you, 97
Things, 87
Think Before You Shoot, 31
Think, now: if you have found a dead bird,
29
This darkness has a quality, 24
This house is floored with water, 30
This is a story. Dear Clive, 92
This is the front door. You can just see, 185
This is the time of year when people die, 200
This tender 'V' of thighs below my window,
264
This truth-telling is well enough, 100
This Ungentle Music, 129
This Winifred Nicholson card for my mother's
birthday, 278
Those thorn trees in your poems, Alistair,
122
Three Rainbows in One Morning, 119
Three times I have slept in your house, 28
Through my pillow, through mattress, carpet,
floor and ceiling, 107
Ting-ting! 'What's in your pocket, sir?' 213
Toads, 196
Today the Dog of Heaven swallowed the
sun, 135
'To Fleur from Pete, on loan perpetual', 162
Tokens, 77
To Marilyn from London, 116
Tongue Sandwiches, 257
Tongue sandwiches on market-day, 257
Too jellied, viscous, floating a condition, 204

Train from the Hook of Holland, 63
Traitors, 252
Trees, 47
Tricks and tumbles are my trade; I'm, 145
Trio, 269
Tunbridge Wells, 172
Turnip-heads, 202
227 Peel Green Road, 236

Under a hedge was good enough for us, 245
Under the Lawn, 197
Under the sand at low tide, 110
Unexpected Visit, 20
Uniunea Scriitorilor, 156

Variations on a Theme of Horace, 103
Viewed from the top, he said, it was like a
wheel, 23
Villa Isola Bella, 139
Visited, 100

Water, 243
We are dried and brittle this morning, 71
Weathering, 124
We awakened facing each other, 89
We bought raspberries in the market, 266
'We did sums at school, Mummy, 166
We give ten pence to the old woman, 108
We three in our dark decent clothes, 189
'Wet the tea, Jinny, the men are back, 66
We weave haunted circles about each other,
40
We went to Malaya for an afternoon, 85
'What are you looking at?' 'Looking', 119
What are you loving me with? I'm dead, 247
What can I have done to earn, 203
What is it, what is it? Quick: that whiff, 206
What May Happen, 193
What shall we do with Granpa, in his silver,
234
What was the creepiest thing about him, 276
When I came in that night I found, 38
When I got up that morning I had no
father, 194
When I went back the school was rather
small, 69
When Laura was born, Ceri watched, 270
When the Americans were bombing Libya,
193
When they were having the Gulf War, 244
When we heard the results of our tests, 265
When you dyed your hair blue, 161
When you're fifteen, no one understands
you, 259
When you were lying on the white sand, 19
Where They Lived, 234

Which redhead did I get my temper from, 242
*Wildlife*, 201
'Will I die?' you ask. And so I enter on, 21
*Willow Creek*, 268
*Witnesses*, 189
*Wren Song*, 198

'You are now walking in the road, 188
You could have called it the year of their
    persecution, 199
You count the fingers first: it's traditional, 192

You did London early, at nineteen, 116
'You'll have to put the little girl down', 140
'You need a bolster,' said the nurse, strap-
    ping a roll, 278
You recognise a body by its blemishes, 52
You're glad I like the chiffonier. But I, 158
Your villa, Katherine, but not your room,
    139
Your 'wedge of stubborn particles', 96
You see your nextdoor neighbour from
    above, 183

**Fleur Adcock** was born in New Zealand but spent part of her childhood in England, returning to live in London in 1963. She was educated at a number of schools and at Victoria University, Wellington, where she obtained an MA with first class honours in Classics. She worked as a librarian until 1979, when she resigned to become a freelance writer.

She has held several literary fellowships, and was Northern Arts Literary Fellow in Newcastle and Durham in 1979-81. She has attended major festivals and given readings of her poetry in the UK and abroad. After her first visit to Romania in 1984 she began learning the language, and has published translations of work by two Romanian poets, as well as translations from medieval Latin poetry in *The Virgin & the Nightingale* (Bloodaxe Books, 1983). She has written libretti for an opera and other works by the composer Gillian Whitehead, and edited several anthologies, including *The Faber Book of Twentieth Century Women's Poetry*.

She has published ten books of poetry, as well as three pamphlets. Her *Selected Poems* was published by OUP in 1983, and a collected edition of her work, *Poems 1960-2000*, by Bloodaxe Books in 2000.

She has received several awards, including a Cholmondeley Award in 1976 and a New Zealand National Book Award in 1984. She is a Fellow of the Royal Society of Literature, and was awarded an OBE in 1996.